AM I A WOMAN?

Am I a Woman?

A Skeptic's Guide to Gender

CYNTHIA ELLER

Beacon Press

BOSTON

Beacon Press
25 Beacon Street
Boston, Massachusetts 02108-2892
www.beacon.org

Beacon Press books
are published under the auspices of
the Unitarian Universalist Association of Congregations.

07 06 05 04 03 8 7 6 5 4 3 2 1

This book is printed on acid-free paper that meets the uncoated paper
ANSI/NISO specifications for permanence as revised in 1992.

Composition by Wilsted & Taylor Publishing Services

Library of Congress Cataloging-in-Publication Data
Eller, Cynthia (Cynthia Lorraine)
    Am I a woman? : a skeptic's guide to gender / Cynthia Eller.
        p. cm.
Includes bibliographical references.
    ISBN 0-8070-7508-6 (alk. paper)
    1. Feminist theory. 2. Sex role. 3. Sex differences (Psychology) I. Title.
    HQ1190.E424 2003
    305.42'01—dc21
                                                    2003002564

FOR LUCY AND SOPHIE

CONTENTS

AM I A WOMAN?

What Is a Woman?

The other day, I was at a sixth-birthday party for a little girl named Zoe. The event was a refreshing break from the usual round of face-painting and gymnastics that are the highlight of single-digit birthday parties here in suburban New Jersey. The entertainment was in the form of a herpetologist in her mid-twenties named Karen. Karen had many snakes to show, and plenty to tell about where they live and what they eat, and anything else the kids were curious to know.

The kids were always curious about one thing: "Is it a boy or a girl?" they asked relentlessly of each and every animal. Karen always gave them an answer, but she kept referring to the scaly things as "he," whatever their actual sex—something the kids kept correcting her on.

At the climax of her show, Karen pulled out an eleven-foot albino python. It was really something to behold, with its pink eyes and its forked tongue thrashing frenetically in and out. "Is it a boy or a girl?" came the by now routine query.

"It's a girl," Karen replied.

This time, however, that answer was inadequate for at least one inquiring six-year-old mind. "How can you tell?" a child asked.

Frankly, I wasn't sure I wanted to know. But I awaited enlightenment along with everyone else, hoping it wouldn't be too gross when it came. Karen walked her way hand-over-hand down several feet of python until she came to a little flap on the snake's underside, about three-quarters down its length.

"See this?" she said. "Boy snakes have two little hooks on either side, called 'spurs.' This snake doesn't have them, so she's a girl."

I have no spurs, nor do I have their human equivalents (would that be testicles, or a penis?), so I guess I'm a girl. Given that I'm in my forties now, that I've borne two children and menstruated dozens upon dozens of times, I think we can just say "woman" and be done with it.

But am I really a woman? I haven't always been so sure. There are a lot of things women are supposed to be and say and do and feel: whip up an amazing casserole with nothing but bread crumbs and cream of mushroom soup; apply lipstick perfectly, quickly, and discreetly without benefit of a mirror; weep affectingly when the heroine of a made-for-television movie-of-the-week discovers her precious only child is afflicted with a rare metabolic disorder. Some of these things women are supposed to be and say and do and feel come very naturally to me. Like I can't throw a ball more than a couple of body lengths, even in a stiff tailwind. Tell me I throw like a girl, and I'll have no grounds to contradict you.

There are other things though that I have had to work at. For instance, playing dumb was a painfully acquired skill (a necessary one, of course, because I wanted boys—and girls too—to like me). I can do it now whenever I want: I just flip the switch, and I'm, like, totally a Valley Girl. But it wasn't always so easy. On numerous other counts of femaleness, I've decided at some point to throw in the towel. Maybe I'm betraying the social insensitivity that's supposed to characterize the male of the species, but it's more than I can gracefully manage to keep track of everyone's birthdays and send each person of my acquaintance an appropriately amusing and affectionate greeting card that magically arrives in their mailbox on the proper date.

When you weigh it all up, on a scale of one to ten, man to woman, I'm not a three. But I'm way short of an eight most of the time. I don't know, maybe I can cop an eight on a really femme day, but most of the time I'd be lucky to get a six, and some days I think I just may have slid under that magic number five.

Which means what? That I'm a man?

You're probably thinking this is a ridiculous question. "Am I a woman?" appears to have all the earmarks of Philosophy 101 queries like "Does the world exist?" "What is beauty?" and the ever popular "If a tree falls in the forest, and no one is there to hear it, does it make a sound?" These are questions that are the stuff of cartoons in *The New Yorker.* Undergraduates may be brought to a reluctant, temporary consideration of them in general ed courses; a self-selected few are captivated by them for a lifetime. But for most people, the obvious answer to questions like these is "who cares?" Come on ... the answer is right there. Am I a woman? Drop pants, take a look, answer received.

But "am I a woman?" is a more personal, painful question than others of its type, and one I think that many if not most women ask themselves in one form or another at critical points in their lives. Women are judged all the time—and judge themselves—as to how well they manifest their supposedly natural inborn femininity. Though it may rarely take the form of the most radical question (am I a woman?), this self-doubt approaches it with questions like "Am I a good enough woman (wife/daughter/mother/friend)?" "Am I as feminine as my best friend (sister/mother/coworker/stranger on the train)?" or at its most piercing level, "What's wrong with me anyway?"

I was raised during the 1960s, when big things were happening for women. Everything about femaleness was getting shaken up, or so it seemed. Women were having premarital sex without apology, they were picketing for job equity, and soap operas were trying out daring new plot lines involving the perilous and thrilling lives of "liberated" women. Of course, I was in grammar school. Things trickled down, but only so far. I kept my eyes and ears open; I sniffed at changes in the wind. And I wore dresses to school every day (except when we went on field trips, and girls were permitted to wear pants), yearned to be one of the popular girls, and dreamed of growing up and becoming a mother. I wrote my fictional children's names in the front of my notebook. I'd barely begun my life, and the height of possibility seemed to me to be the opportunity of giving life—and a name—to someone else.

And yet for reasons I can't recall, when I learned in second grade that no woman had ever been president of the United States, I announced my intention to be the first.

I assume I said it to provoke a reaction in people, because once it lost its shock value, I quit talking about it. Besides, I began to figure out that claiming a desire to be president wasn't going to endear me with the popular girls.

Four years later, when I graduated from George Ellery Hale Elementary School, the class mothers (no fathers on the horizon back then—and darned few today, for that matter) put together a slide show in which each child was featured in turn, their school picture head shot pasted onto a caricatured figure accompanied with text describing their successful adult lives. I waited for my slide to appear, closing my eyes and praying for mercy. "How bad could it be?" I tried to reassure myself. Finally it arrived. My funny little head, with my bangs half grown in and my teeth sticking out at odd angles, sat atop the figure of a leggy woman in an orange pantsuit with a leopard-trim scarf around her neck. She was holding a briefcase. "Cynthia Eller," it read, "first woman president of the United States."

The class howled with laughter. I wished myself invisible or dead or maybe both. I remember being especially furious with the moms. How could they be so cruel as to parrot back to my classmates some foolish thing I had said four years earlier when I didn't know any better, when I was a mere child? Only seven years old? (Now when I reflect on this, I think of how much work the moms put into the slide show and I marvel at my ingratitude.)

Last week on the way to school, my daughter told me that anyone can grow up to be president of the United States. "Really, Mommy," she insisted, while I demurred, thinking of immigrants and other such exceptions, along with the lengthy list of improbables: African Americans, women, Asian Americans, Muslims, Jews, Latinos ... you name it. "I could even grow up to be president," Sophie said.

"Yes," I agreed, smiling to myself, "maybe you'll be the first woman president."

This made Sophie very happy. I tightened my hands on the steering wheel and fought off the impulse to warn her not to say anything like this out loud to her little friends, or god forbid, to their mothers. Because maybe things will be different for her.

Obviously, I haven't grown up to be president. On the other hand, I've never been the housewife and mother of five I anticipated becoming. At age forty-two, with two young children and a full-time job, I think I can safely say that I never will. I now imagine the prospect of marrying young and staying home with my five children with the fascinated dread and horror of one who slams on her brakes just inches from a ten-car pileup on the freeway.

I suppose I've ended up somewhere in the middle, like most women of my generational cohort. Like others, I've been tremendously influenced by the feminist movement. I've demanded a life that is interesting and full, one that minimizes time spent wearing high heels or folding my husband's underwear. But I've also, over the years, tried to avoid being seen as the sixth-grade girl who aspires to the United States presidency, or the teenager who would rather go for a walk than experiment with eyelash curlers, or the new mother who finds breastfeeding her infant considerably less rewarding than, say, mowing the lawn.

This causes me to wonder: if being a woman is simply a matter of what genitalia I'm sporting, why has it been so hard to pull it off gracefully? If I sprang from the womb genetically programmed to be sweet and considerate toward people, then why did I have to pore over my sister's copy of *Here's to You, Miss Teen* to learn how to encourage a boy to talk about his own interests when out on a date? And why have there been so many missteps along the way? For something so apparently natural as my sex, femaleness has turned out to be a depressingly huge and tiresome identity to carry around. Sure, I've enjoyed it sometimes; a lot of times. But when it stops being enjoyable, it's not like it goes away. By now I've forged an identity for myself, femaleness and all, that suits me rather well without involving a lot of what feels to me like artifice. Still, I spent many years trying to figure out how to be an acceptable girl/woman and worrying that I might not be up to the task.

Of course, I think women are set up to doubt ourselves, and in particular, to doubt our adequacy as women. Keeping us perpetually off-balance undercuts our attempts to address sex-based injustices. We fret over our job or our family or our hair as if they were our own personal crosses to bear without pausing to recognize that our jobs and our families and our hair—and the way we are trained to think about them—are very wrapped up in arbitrary ideas about who women are or are supposed to be. For behind the intensely personal torment of asking "am I a woman?" lies another, logically prior question: "What is a woman?" The first question sounds quirky, individual; the second is profoundly political. Why? Because it's not a matter of idle curiosity who gets put in which camp, male or female. It's not like dividing people up on the basis of whether their last names begin with a letter between A and M or one between N and Z. Whether you're designated female or male has an enormous impact on what sort of life you can lead, what opportunities will or will not be presented to you, what people will expect of you. That realization, and the belief that this situation is unjust, is for me a bottom line definition of feminism—not the only definition, but a very basic one.

But feminists are not the only ones who care about what a woman is. Everyone does, as near as I can tell. I have yet to meet a person who doesn't have an opinion about how women and men are different and why. Television talk shows and self-help best-sellers, for example, are a virtual orgy of debate around these questions. Indeed, I don't think a single day goes by in my life in which someone, somewhere does not make some statement of the form "it's a guy thing" or "it's because she's a girl, you don't get that with boys." Radio, television, lunchtime conversation, board meeting, kindergarten field trip, you name it, the topic of gender pops up. Yes, I'm hypersensitive to these kinds of comments because I teach and do research in women's studies. But put up your radar for a day and see if I'm not right. Gender talk is absolutely everywhere. Religious fundamentalists carefully articulate the different roles God has ordained for the two sexes. Biologists and geneticists seek to demonstrate differences between the sexes and explain them via biochemical mechanisms. Politicians, liberal and conservative, strive to make social policy based on what they believe the differing needs, wants, and aspirations of women and men are. People don't agree about what a woman is, but they all seem to have a stake in the answer.

Amid all this debate, there does seem to be one intriguing point of agreement. When we say that a person is a man or a woman, we are actually talking about two intermixed but analytically separable things: *sex* and *gender.* Sex is biological, factual, unchangeable (or changeable only through excesses of biological and surgical engineering that most people find unsavory to contemplate). Gender, on the other hand, is the product of social mores and customs, of childhood training and social policy. It is comparatively easily changed. It is less "real" than sex.

I think it has to count as a triumph of the feminist movement that this distinction is well accepted by people on all stations of the political spectrum. It was a basic feminist point, forged to sometimes iron hardness in the 1970s, that there are people who have vaginas and breasts and who bear the next generation in their wombs (people whose sex is female), but that this need not mean that such people could not be senators or construction workers (professions which, by historical accident, have been "gendered" male). This is not a terribly controversial assertion anymore, though it was just a scant few decades ago.

People don't agree as to just which traits are biological and which are cultural, which are "sex" and which are "gender." Some would tell you, for example, that men are physiologically predisposed toward thoughtlessness, which is why they leave the toilet seat up, while others will say that men in a male-dominant society are trained to think of themselves as little princes, and that's why they "forget" about the comfort and convenience of others who share their bathrooms. There are also divergent views on which culturally created gender roles are socially beneficial and which are not. Many people, for example, will be happy to explain to you why women should not be senators or construction workers even though they are biologically capable of taking on those roles and performing them well. Still, most people agree that there are these two components to a person's identity as male or female, man or woman: the given (sex), and the created (gender).

Just as American culture has come to a consensus on this matter, however, academic gender theory has undercut it. Sex is no more "real," no less cultural, current theorists say, than gender. Yes, bodies have parts, and not everyone's parts are identical. But our labeling of certain bodies as female and others as male is a cultural invention. As such, this labeling is susceptible to the same sorts of ideological biases and scientific mistakes as any other distinction we could care to draw between persons. Sex can change, just as gender can, as soon as we begin to think about it and categorize it and enact it in different ways. There is no stable biological ground resting under the cultural maelstroms of gender. Sex is gender; gender is sex. All is flux.

Now *this* little nugget of gender theory has not translated into the cultural mainstream very well at all. It hasn't had as long to infuse popular consciousness as the old sex/gender distinction, but I have serious doubts as to how well it will, even given a comparable period of time. It's extremely counterintuitive. Biological sex has to count as one of the more obvious facts of nature, alongside phenomena like gravity and the changing of the seasons. When I drop a stone off a bridge into a pond, is it a set of culturally constructed beliefs about nature that makes the stone splash when it hits the water? If we had constructed our understandings of the world differently, would the stone vanish quietly or hover in midair or possibly launch up into the stratosphere? The conviction that one shouldn't wear white after Labor Day is culturally constructed, but surely it has nothing to do with human fashion customs that it starts to get colder after Labor Day in the temperate regions of the northern hemisphere.

I'm actually partial to the theory that sex is every bit as constructed as gender. In fact, unless I call it "biological sex," I'll be using the terms *sex* and *gender* interchangeably. Its counterintuitive nature notwithstanding, the theory that sex and gender are both culturally constructed is quite elegant; it is beautifully self-consistent and more relevant to the world in which we live than you might think. But I have no serious hopes of mainstreaming the idea that the sex/gender distinction is pointless, that biological sex is a product of how we think about and categorize things rather than a fact in itself.

Fortunately, this causes me no despair. I don't think we need this theory to move forward as feminists, and that's my primary goal. As any journalist will tell you, the feminist movement is now moribund, or at least is not its rocking and rolling former self. I worry that one of the reasons for this has to do with internal and seemingly endless debates around the nature of sex and gender. Answers to the question "what is a woman?" run the gamut among self-described feminists, just as they do in the population at large. Depending on which feminists you listen to, women are the natural nurturers and civilizers of the human race from time immemorial; a group of people with similar biological capacities (such as menstruation and childbirth) that yield similar psychological states; individuals who share the same sex as their primary caregiver; an oppressed economic class; or a convenient (for systems of male dominance) fiction that is taught by one generation to the next, whose members must then teach it to their children in order for the fiction to survive. Or possibly all of these.

Back and forth we argue. The debate is more fascinating and downright fun than you might imagine, especially if you're not into that kind of thing. Yet we rarely seem to get anywhere, and the rift between academic and popular feminism—or, perhaps, the empty space in popular culture where feminism should be—continues to widen.

It's a truism that many women who are committed to equality and fairness for women and girls would shudder to call themselves feminists. The woman whose boss keeps telling her dirty jokes after she has politely asked him to stop is not a feminist; she just wants him to knock it off. The woman who is campaigning for equal funding for boys' and girls' soccer teams is not a feminist; she just wants equal treatment for her daughter. The woman who falls into bed exhausted every night after working an eight-hour day and then helping her kids with their homework and cooking dinner and washing dishes and paying the bills is not a feminist; she just wants her husband to get up off the couch and help her once in a while.

Who are the people who call themselves feminists then? For the most part, the media depict them the same way they did in the early 1970s: feminists are shrill, bitter, masculine-looking, humorless, man-hating women (and probably lesbians to boot) who begrudge other women their lipstick because they're so badly adjusted to their own gender. Now that feminism has taken root in women's studies programs at American universities nationwide, there's a variant stereotype of feminists emerging: they are humorless, pedantic academics who say manifestly absurd things like "sex is nothing but the cultural construct of a patriarchal society."

I very much want to see bridges built between women who resist applying the term *feminist* to themselves and all us self-proclaimed feminists busily bemoaning the false consciousness of "ordinary" women, whom we see as the unwitting victims of patriarchy. In other words, I bring a very pragmatic concern to the question "what is a woman?" I want to know not just what femaleness is, but also which way of defining femaleness is most likely to bring the feminist movement to vibrant life, where it can be instrumental in addressing sex-based injustices and calling for change.

For these purposes, I think we need a definition of femaleness that doesn't make the people categorized as such feel they have to do any overhauling of their bodies or personalities. That is, I don't want anyone to worry that her femininity is not up to snuff—or, just as bad, to feel that she can't possibly be a feminist because she is too feminine, likes being at home with her young children, or loves men and doesn't feel that they are the root of all evil. I want a definition of femaleness that allows women (and men too) of different races, classes, nationalities, sexual orientations, and so on to make common cause with one another when the situation merits it. I want a definition of femaleness that is easy to grasp, that doesn't require mastery of a complicated and jargon-filled discourse. Finally, I want a definition of femaleness that acknowledges and respects the fact that most of us don't suffer any serious confusion over who's a man and who's a woman when we're in any kind of social setting, whether that be an airport waiting room or an office party.

In this quest for a definition of femaleness that can make good sense and advance the feminist cause, we needn't start from scratch. There are many ways of thinking about femaleness, of answering the question "what is a woman?" that have been around for anywhere from twenty-five hundred to ten years. These formulations have been hugely influential for everyone (whether they're consciously aware of it or not) from highbrow academics to feminist activists, from your favorite aunt to the usher at your local movie theater. I haven't invented these theories, and many descriptions of them exist in texts on feminist theory or gender theory or the psychology of sex difference. Unfortunately, they are usually delivered in, at best, academic prose, and at worst, completely obtuse language that only the initiated can decipher. I want to keep it simple here. But as we search for a compelling definition of femaleness, what options are already available, how well do they capture our experience of femaleness, and how usable are they as tools to address sex-based injustice?

In general, theories of what femaleness is cluster around three potential markers: physiology, feelings, and behavior. Each of these markers is used at different times and places and in various ways to determine who is male or female, and more, what maleness and femaleness themselves are.

First physiology: women are supposed to have certain physical characteristics. This is probably the most commonsense answer to the question "what is a woman?" A woman is someone with female primary and secondary sex characteristics. You can *see* them. But physiology is also the key criterion for many more sophisticated theories of gender determination. Physicians and biologists have been making arguments about what makes a person a man or a woman for many centuries now. They haven't always agreed with one another, but they have repeatedly gone back to the body as the locus of sex. The ancient Greeks attributed sex difference to bodily heat: women were colder than men, which is why their sexual organs did not develop "fully" (that is, externally). Scientists today tend to think sex is fundamentally related to the configuration of our chromosomes, perhaps with some other physiological traits factoring in as well. Either way, the existence of sexed physiological characteristics is one way to determine who is and is not a woman.

But there are other ways people think about the nature of femaleness. Women are defined by their feelings, by the kind of emotions they have, the way they interact with others, and the way they conceive of themselves in relationship to others and to the world in general. Surely this is one way that popular culture distinguishes women from men, one method we use to decide if a person is feminine (as a woman is or should be) or masculine (as a man is or should be). Women are sensitive and emotional, and good at perceiving and dealing with the psychological subtleties of interpersonal situations. Explanations for exactly what these psychological characteristics are and how women come to have them are a crucial part of many theories that purport to tell us what a woman is. Women, like men, it is said, negotiate their gender identity through the interplay of their relationships to same- and different-sexed parents. Because women are the same sex as their mothers (and not their fathers), this creates in women a specific sort of identity, a feminine one. If women— that is, biological females, defined by Freud as people lacking a penis—do not manifest this feminine identity, something has gone wrong. They are, perhaps, psychologically male, in a way that can be contrary to their physiological sex. In other words, maleness and femaleness may have their source in physiology— it is your genitals, typically, that cause you to identify with one parent or another—but it is the interplay of physiology and family environment that really creates male and female persons as we know them.

Another way we commonly decide if a person is a woman is by watching how she or he behaves. These behaviors range from the mundane (women cross their legs when they sit down) to the sublime (women light up at the sight of an infant, any infant). You don't need to be an academic gender theorist to know that women and men act differently, or even to speculate about why they do. Our behavior is an integral part of how we position ourselves in the world as male or female. But there are gender theories that make behavior the trump card for any gender de- termination. It's how people act that makes them what they are: female or male. Even more, it's how people act that makes fe- maleness and maleness what they are. It is the behaviors them- selves, from whatever source they derive, that constitute the phenomenon of gender.

"What is a woman?" is a fascinating question with a range of possible answers. But I don't want to stray too far here from the first question I raised: "Am I a woman?" hits close to home. It brings what can be some very abstract and obscure debates down here to where the rubber hits the road, where each of us works out her own sense of herself in concert with the world around her. As the grounding dictum of the feminist movement states, the personal is the political. By starting with myself (arguably the person I know best) and examining the nature of my femaleness, of my femininity or lack thereof, I stand to learn a lot about what we collectively think femaleness is and what kind of impact that can have on a person's life.

I start with myself for another reason too. It has become fashionable lately (at least in the trendy academic circles I sometimes call home) to "deconstruct" gender, as I will be doing here. People of many different sorts conduct this exercise: it is not limited to feminists, or to gays and lesbians, or even to poststructural literary critics who have devoted a significant amount of time to reading Jacques Derrida in the original French (for whom deconstruction is the most exciting thing to come down the turnpike in the entire intellectual history of Western civilization). What these varied groups and individuals share in common might most simply be called a stance of "antiessentialism." Together they argue that there is no single trait or characteristic (or no group of traits or characteristics) that is "essentially" female, that by itself definitively captures the essence of womanhood.

The favorite, indeed the most obvious case studies for such a deconstructive exercise are transgendered and transsexual people,[*] those individuals who have put in time on both sides of the gender divide. The transgendered live in the land of drag queens, diesel dykes, and surgically swapped sex organs, that place on the gender map where femaleness shades over into maleness and vice versa. Through their very lives, the transgendered stand poised to put the definition of womanness into the

---

[*] *Transsexual* is the generally accepted term for individuals who have changed their sex through surgery and/or hormones and wish to fully inhabit the sex of their choosing rather than the one to which they were born. *Transgendered* is a newer term, usually meant to describe individuals who identify with a gender other than their biological sex, though they may never have surgery or take hormones to bring their physiology in line with their chosen gender. *Transgender* is also applied more loosely to all those who feel themselves to somehow transcend the binary categories of gender whether for reasons of sexuality, physiology, or gender identity.

magician's coffinlike black box, wave a wand over her, and make her disappear. Poof! Gender loses its essence, the categories are undone, and maleness and femaleness scatter all over the map and indeed right over the edge into uncharted territory like so many cockroaches seeking any available haven when the overhead light flicks on. Transgendered individuals see themselves in much this way: they are the lawless nomads in the distant Wild West of the gender wars, those who make bold to proclaim themselves *Gender Outlaws* (the title of a book by male-to-female transsexual Kate Bornstein) or *Transgender Warriors* (the title of a book by born-female-now-transgendered Leslie Feinberg), those who are ready to move *Beyond Pink and Blue* (the subtitle of Feinberg's book *Trans Liberation*) and who aspire to *Sexual Subversion and the End of Gender* (the subtitle of a book by male-to-female transsexual Riki Anne Wilchins).

What does this have to do with the rest of us? A lot, for anyone who cares to speculate upon just what makes a person an honest-to-God, card-carrying woman. Is a male-to-female transsexual a woman? If so, where does s/he cross the line? Putting on women's clothing? Walking unnoticed into the women's restroom? Living "as a woman" for some set number of years? Taking female hormones? Having his/her penis removed? Getting a surgically constructed vulva? Why at one point and not at another? Really, the answer isn't at all clear. That's what makes the question so interesting, so arresting. Sensible people can disagree.

"Am I a woman?" even retains a bit of its uncertainty in the writings of lesbians, gays, bisexuals, and others keen on "queering" gender. Is the butch lesbian a woman? Well, yes, she is, if not in exactly the way that other women are women. By some criteria she's indisputably a woman ("does she have a vagina?"), but by others ("does she walk 'like a woman'?") it isn't so clear. Again, there's room for doubt and discussion among sensible people (though not perhaps so much as when the question is asked of a transsexual).

But when I ask if I personally am a woman, the stakes are

shifted. Because let me tell you, *everyone* thinks I am a woman. If there are people who can noncontroversially be called women, then I'm one of them. I'm a veritable stereotype of normative femaleness: two X chromosomes, classically female body morphology, heterosexual; not to mention white and middle-class and married-with-children, living in a three-bedroom single-family dwelling in suburbia.

Of course, none of these latter characteristics should go toward making me believably female: women come in all races and classes and sexual orientations, and live in all sorts of homes and family arrangements. But if you call up a mental image of the archetypal middle-aged American woman, say the one who appears in sitcoms and television commercials for frozen pizzas and cold medicines and sanitary napkins, that's me! If I'm not a woman, then who is?

This is just the point. If the naturalness and obviousness of my gender can be called into question, that's significant. When transgendered people articulate their experiences, the margins of the gender divide bleed into one another and things begin to look hazy. I like to think that when people like me articulate our experiences, we can see just as clearly that the center does not hold.

Friends have noted that this question—"am I a woman?"—bears a strong resemblance to another feminist question, a very famous one: "Ain't I a woman?" That question was posed by Sojourner Truth, an African-American ex-slave who lived in the nineteenth century and worked as an activist for the abolitionist and feminist causes. In a justly famous speech delivered in 1851 to a women's rights convention in Akron, Ohio, Sojourner Truth challenged her male hecklers with these words:

> That man over there says that women need to be helped into carriages, and lifted over ditches, and to have the best place everywhere. Nobody ever helps me into carriages, or over mud-puddles, or gives me any best place! And ain't I a woman? Look at me! Look at my arm! I have ploughed and planted, and gathered into barns, and no man could head me! And ain't I a woman? I could work as

much and eat as much as a man—when I could get it—and bear the lash as well! And ain't I a woman? I have borne thirteen children, and seen them most all sold off to slavery, and when I cried out with my mother's grief, none but Jesus heard me! And ain't I a woman?

I don't presume to be any sort of contemporary counterpart for Sojourner Truth, but there's a basic similarity in our questions. Sojourner Truth challenges standard definitions of femaleness from her position outside of them, arguing that these definitions can't be very accurate if they so obviously fail to include her and her experiences. I'm trying to unsettle these same definitions (albeit a hundred and fifty years later) from my position inside of them, arguing that if I, who am *supposed* to fit into this category, do so in such an imperfect manner, then maybe the category itself is flawed.

I'm not the archetypal female, of course, or even the stereotypical one, my superficial similarity to television moms notwithstanding. Probably the clearest sign that I'm not the stereotypical woman is my inability to just leave well enough alone and agree with everyone else that I am a woman. I realize that not everybody could work up a good case of angst over their reputed sex when there are so many other things to do and think about in life. But that I would push and prod at the contours of my gender identity makes perfect sense once you know a bit about me.

When I was in graduate school I had a roommate who was in the full flower of a fascination with the occult. This extended to an interest in dreams and dream interpretation. When we were living together, he was recording as many of his dreams as he could remember and quizzing me about mine when I stumbled into the kitchen each morning to get a cup of coffee. Once he asked me if I saw any general theme in my dreams, features that occurred night after night on my inner movie screen. To my surprise, there *was* such a theme tying together the strange places and twisted plots that popped up in my dreams every night. I was almost always with large groups of people, far away from home, at a conference or retreat, or with a tribe that was making its way through some postapocalyptic scenario. The landscapes changed on a nightly basis, as did the specific people I was with. Every night was another world premiere, another first screening. But the psychic content, the way the "I" character of this dream felt, was alarmingly consistent: I spent my dream time trying to figure out how I was supposed to act. The rules were different in this place, among these people, wherever it was. Everyone else, even if they were migrants like me, seemed to effortlessly absorb and live by the relevant social rules without giving it a second thought. I knew that I appeared to function about as well as anyone else in these social groups, but my approach was entirely different. They were making their way to appropriate behavior by an instantaneous, intuitive gnosis. I was getting there by a plodding, laborious process of observing other people, mimicking them, and then watching how others reacted to my imitation so I could fine-tune it for future deployment. It was as though we were all learning a language, but while others magically caught on and began to speak like natives, I was returning to my hut at night to pore over vocabulary lists, to write down everything I'd heard and try to puzzle out underlying schemes and hidden grammars so that I could more easily formulate the correct sentences at the proper time.

I didn't need access to my roommate's library of esotericism to figure out what that theme meant. It was simply a nighttime reiteration of how my waking life felt all the time: like trying to navigate in a foreign country with only my intellect to assist me.

Yet even if the process I've experienced of learning to be a woman, like learning a new language, feels more self-conscious and labored to me than it does to others, I continue to believe that others are going through the same process nevertheless. I'm hoping then that my inability to take things at face value can be turned to advantage in this inquiry into the nature of femaleness and the political implications of defining it in one way rather than another.

CHAPTER 2

Under the Axis:
The Physiology of Sex

How often are you seriously confronted by someone whose sex isn't immediately obvious to you? I'll bet it's not often. I have only to look out my window for confirmation on this point. My office faces a busy downtown street and a train station. Everyone is in motion out there, so I'll have to do this fast, but right now I'm looking at nine people. Five are women, three are men, and one is, I think, an adolescent boy, or maybe a girl, or possibly a small, really butch woman who dresses like a guy. So, let's see ... that's a total of nine, of which eight can be confidently identified as to sex. You have to factor in my myopia. I bet if I walked right up to that one person whose sex wasn't immediately obvious to me, I'd be able to identify him/her as well, in one of those great gestalt assessments that we human beings can make in mere fragments of seconds (the legacy of all those millennia of protohuman jungle living, no doubt, where the ability to distinguish friends from enemies, predators from lunch, had, as we latter-day knee-jerk Darwinians like to say, "survival value"). I bet I could sit here looking out the window all day and never find my sex-identification skills seriously challenged.

But wait ... hold on ... there's a person walking out of the ice cream store: blue hospital scrubs, face mask dangling around the neck, short Afro, moving in an utterly innocuous ice-cream-eating saunter.... Male or female? I'm not sure! How fabulous that this indefinite-sex body in blue scrubs should be walking down the sidewalk at this very moment, just as I settle in to write about the obviousness of physical sex! How perfectly unexpected and wonderful!

Oh, hold on a minute—this person is stepping up from behind a low wall; I'm getting the full frontal. . . . Wow, look at the size of those feet! Female or male, this person has been shopping in the men's shoe department.

It's all moot. Mr. Blue Scrubs is no more than thirty feet from my window now. He's a guy. Serious five o'clock shadow.

Of course, I haven't been taking the possibility of deception into account. Could I be fooled by a cunningly dressed man trying to look like a woman? By a woman trying to look like a man? Definitely. A lot of what I'm noticing here is clothes, which, unisex fashions notwithstanding, are usually dead giveaways as to which sex a person is trying to appear to be. So let's leave the people on the street behind and get down to the nitty-gritty: to what people look like with their clothes *off*. If it has a penis, it's a man. If it doesn't, it's a woman. It couldn't be easier. The three-year-olds at my baby daughter's day care center will tell you this. "Boys have penises," they lisp. "Girls don't." (In this progressive era, children are rarely taught to resort to euphemism.)

But let's say that you have yourself a little boy, complete with penis. You decide to have him circumcised. The doctor—who, for the sake of argument, is none too coordinated—makes a mistake and the whole thing gets amputated. Don't think this can't happen. It has. If you don't like that scenario, take another page from real life and tweak it ever so slightly. What if Lorena Bobbitt, when asked what she'd done with her husband's penis, said that she'd rather not reveal that information? Or lied and said that she'd thrown it out the car window three blocks away from where she'd actually disposed of it? John Wayne Bobbitt and his equipment would never have been surgically reunited. Is the victim of a too-enthusiastic circumcision (his real-life name was Bruce Reimer) still a boy? Is the man whose penis has been lopped off by a vengeful wife (or rape victim) still a man?

It seems to me that John Wayne Bobbitt, sans penis, is still a man. A singularly unfortunate man, perhaps, but still a man. With Bruce Reimer, it's less clear. In 1967, when he was almost two years old, Reimer's doctors (with the permission of his parents) finished up what they'd inadvertently started, doing it more neatly this time. They crafted a new set of genitalia for Bruce that didn't involve any protuberances. The Reimers took Bruce—now Brenda—home, and raised him/her as a girl. Ten years later, was Brenda a boy without a penis whose parents sent him out of the house in drag every day? Or was Brenda a girl? If she was a girl, was she a regular girl, or some special kind of girl? If she was a special kind of girl, how would you know that without knowing the history of her case? No one was advertising the business of Brenda's infant sex change. Brenda herself didn't know about it. How could you dream of calling a person like that a boy? A child without a penis, dressed like a girl, believing she is a girl, going to Girl Scout meetings along with her peers?

Actually, Brenda didn't take too well to femaleness. At age fourteen, she discovered her history, stopped taking estrogen supplements, and had herself switched over to play on the other team, renaming herself David in an effort to get a fresh start. This would seem to move David Reimer into the John Wayne Bobbitt category of "male comma, unfortunate." But David Reimer was socialized as a female. What stands in the way of saying that at age ten anyway, in the midst of the Brenda years, he was a she?

Ignoring his later return to maleness, one possible reason for deeming Brenda not-female would be that he was born with a penis, just like John Wayne Bobbitt. It was only through accident or violence that both were detached from the usual sign of their maleness.

This may hold true for Reimer and Bobbitt, but there are individuals who are born without penises—sometimes with more or less serviceable-looking vulvas—only to grow them at puberty as they gradually move from large clitoris to small penis and beyond. Usually socialized as girls, when confronted with their very own penis, these individuals typically cross over gender lines and grow up to be men. Here it would seem that the penis indeed makes the man, Reimer and Bobbitt notwithstanding.

However, sex researchers will usually say that these "penis-at-twelve" individuals were always male, even as infants, in spite of their apparent vulvas and their gender socialization. Why? Because they have XY chromosomes. A hereditary inability to process DHT (dihydrotestosterone) while in utero resulted in children who combined female external genitalia with male internal genitalia. You take a look between their legs, you think female. That's about as far as most new parents, or even doctors, have reason to look. But inside are testicles. And at puberty, with a fresh surge of plain old testosterone, their external genitalia come into alignment with their internal genitalia, and they seem to be male in every respect. They can even go on to father children.

So do the chromosomes make the man? It is often suggested that an XY genetic code is a one-way ticket to maleness, as demonstrated in a recent mapping of the Y chromosome (see figure 2.1). But there are a couple of problems with relying on chromosomes for sex identification. First is the existence of additional configurations of sex chromosomes outside the two we think of most often, female (XX) and male (XY): things like Klinefelter's Syndrome (XXY) and Turner's Syndrome (X), XYY syndrome, and trisomies and tetrasomies like XXX and XXXY. There are even people known as "mosaics" who have two genetic codes that manifest in different body cells. In some cases, one set of DNA is XY and the other XX. Does that elusive Y chromosome make such a person a man?

Complicating this picture further is the fact that people with unusually configured sex chromosomes invariably get raised as either girls or boys. Whatever their peculiar mix of sex chromosomes, they typically grow genitalia that appear to be either male or female, making it comparatively easy for parents to announce that little Joe or Josephine has arrived, and that tiny

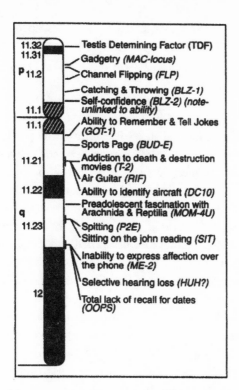

FIGURE 2.1
A humorous mapping of the Y chromosome by geneticist Jane Gitschier.

rugby suits or hair bows will soon be required. Indeed, in many cases neither the child nor the parents are aware that a chromosomal abnormality exists. Klinefelter's and Turner's syndromes both result in a characteristic appearance that is somewhat unusual ("Klinefelter's boys" are somewhat taller than average, have high-pitched voices and sometimes breasts; "Turner's girls" are typically short in stature, with necks that appear webbed and breasts that are widely spaced), and infertility sometimes tips off adults to their XXY or X status. But others with sex chromosome abnormalities look as normal as anyone else and go on to reproduce. I think we'd have to call these individuals women and men. So it can't be the XX versus XY switch that determines who counts as female or male. Complicating things even further are genetic mutations that result in individuals known in the medical literature as "XY females" and "XX males," people whose chromosomal and genital sex don't line up, ever. By one physiological marker they are male; by another they are just as clearly female.

These sex chromosome idiosyncrasies, combined with genital "malformations" (with clinical names like "micropenis") and various hormonal abnormalities (that create things like penis-at-twelve syndrome), are collectively termed *intersex anomalies.* These are way more common than you probably imagine. The first time I read about so-called intersexes was in a feminist context. I thought, "This is a very interesting trip through the freak show, but isn't it kind of pathetic for feminists to behave as though these terribly rare hormonal and chromosomal conditions can stick so much as a tiny pin into the great blimp of biological sex? I mean, come on: it's female and male, vagina and penis, XX and XY 99.99 percent of the time."

But actually "nature" does not produce individuals with matching chromosomes, hormones, and genitalia 99.99 percent of the time. It's more like 96 to 99 percent.* Yes, we're still talking about an overwhelming majority of unambiguous males and females. Chances are that the nine people I spied out my office window this morning were all either male or female, from their chromosomes right down to their privates. But if I were to look out my window all day, it's highly probable that I would see a person (or several people) who had to have a little surgical or hormonal doctoring to steer their chromosomes, hormones, and genitalia into one of our two favorite grooves: male or female. Maybe one of those women I was looking at had a little penis in her panties.

I don't guess that most people with these conditions spend a lot of time discussing them with people they meet in passing. I like to think that my closest women friends would let me know if they had had a penis in days gone by, and no one has ever con-

---

*Estimates for the incidence of intersex births vary from 0.02 percent for specific chromosomal abnormalities to 4 percent for every type of intersex syndrome combined.

fided anything like this to me. On the other hand, last year an old friend dropped by to tell me that she was a lesbian. I never even suspected. The gossip was always that her husband was gay. We, her mutual friends, all worried about how devastated she would be if and when she found out about her husband, given how naive she seemed to be. (Indeed, she claims that she didn't know female homosexuality existed until she was out of college. It wasn't possible, she thought. Who would put what where?) But it turns out her husband has recently gone on to marry another woman and father a child with her, so for now anyway, he appears to be straight. It was she who was crawling under the buffet table to dine on the other side. That same year a friend from high school told me about her husband's infidelities, all with other men. I like to think my gaydar is pretty good, especially when it comes to men, but it had never crossed my mind that he was anything other than a standard-issue heterosexual.

I'm not suggesting that intersex anomalies and homosexuality are linked to one another, or even that they're somehow alike. I'm just saying that your friends don't tell you everything. You may not know them as well as you think you do.

Now I've known well over a hundred people in the course of my life so far. And I've met plenty of people who are in the ninety-ninth percentile for something or other: height, obesity, a great tennis game, whatever. You have to figure I've known some intersexes without, well, *knowing* it. So maybe it's worth considering that you can't decide that a man is a man simply because he has a penis or testicles or a Y chromosome or a generous supply of testosterone.

David Reimer is a man, even though he spent twelve formative years as a girl and the penis he has now had to be crafted surgically. Interestingly, Reimer's case has been used to make all sorts of contradictory arguments about gender. During the Brenda years, his treating psychologist, John Money, reported Reimer's sex change as staggeringly successful, living proof that gender is entirely a matter of socialization. Later, Reimer's decision to be male was a great coup for those who want to believe that when it comes to sex, nature will win over nurture every time (as in the title of the book telling Reimer's story, *As Nature Made Him*). Given that it was written onto every cell of his being, David Reimer couldn't get away from his maleness. No matter what his environment sent his way, whatever means people employed to train him into femininity, down deep he knew that femaleness was a bad fit, a suit of clothes that itched and rubbed and pulled and just never felt right. Score one for biological determination. Chromosomes and hormones always get their day in court.

Except it doesn't always work out that way. Think of George Jorgensen, the first American transsexual to hit the headlines with news of his sex change operation, performed in Denmark in 1952. Jorgensen had a penis well into adulthood. He had testicles. He had a Y chromosome. He produced testosterone and looked convincingly (too convincingly, for his tastes) male. I think we have to agree that physiologically, George was a man. But down deep he knew that maleness was a bad fit, a suit of clothes that itched and rubbed and pulled and just never felt right. If a hidden set of ovaries or an overgrown clitoris or a second X chromosome doesn't account for George's profound desire to become Christine, what does?

I've spent altogether too much time talking about men for someone who has set out to determine what constitutes femaleness. But I think we can safely conclude that the formulaic response of the three-year-old—boys have penises, and girls don't—falls short of the mark. Femaleness cannot be defined as the absence of maleness, with every penis-bearer being a man, and every penis-lacker being a woman.

Is it my vagina, then—rather than my lack of a penis—that makes me a woman? Curiously, the vagina didn't count for much a couple of generations ago. It was the uterus where femaleness happened. "Woman is a womb" was the watchword, the epigrammatic definition of femaleness. As recently as 1949, Simone de Beauvoir began her feminist magnum opus, *The Second Sex*, by citing this woman=womb formulation. This alone makes me wary of the suggestion that either my vagina or my uterus successfully determines my femaleness. First it's one; then it's the other. First it's the uterus (which I take to be code language for reproductive ability); then it's the vagina (which I read as code language for sexual intercourse). All this in the space of a century.

I've always hated the word *vagina*. That long i-sound right in the middle of the word, all by itself, it makes the thing sound vulgar. I don't know why it should, but it does. When I first learned that the territory in between my legs could be broken down into component parts, I was told that boys had penises and girls had vaginas. And it was during this exact same conversation that I learned that boys put their penises in girls' vaginas to make babies. Ergo, the vagina was a hole. It was the nothing where someone else put their something. No wonder I didn't feel thrilled to have one.

I've heard that Eve Ensler chose to call her show *The Vagina Monologues* because she deemed *vagina* to be the only word for women's external genitalia that referred to the entire reproductive/pleasure unit without being derogatory. I never took *vagina* to mean the whole unit. I took it to mean the hole. I've queried many friends on this, and a surprising number, especially men, agree with Ensler: the vagina is the whole unit. But I've recently found my point of view confirmed in my husband's old college textbook, *Biological Science,* third edition, by William T. Keaton. On page 389, there is a diagram of the female reproductive tract (fig. 9-48) in which a cross-sectioned cylinder leading from the outside world to the cervix is labeled "vagina." My copy editor tells me that *vagina* derives from a Latin word for *sheath,* suggesting the vagina is indeed defined by what is expected to go into it (in this case, a penis).

For these reasons and others, I've long preferred the term *vulva* when I want to get clinical about female genitalia. Right from the get-go, I told my older daughter that what she called "the front of her tushie" was rightly known as her "vulva." Damned if "vulva" isn't starting to sound vulgar too. I don't know if it's because *vulva* and *vulgar* share the first three letters, or if it has to with those messy l's and v's in the middle.

In any event, I have a vulva, or a vagina, or whatever you want to call it. I have the whole enchilada, right down to the labia minora. I'm an obvious physiological female, an uncomplicated case. The anatomy checks out, and furthermore, over the years it's managed to perform all its supposed female-specific functions from multiple orgasm to reproduction, and everything else in between.

Not only that, I've been exclusively heterosexual up until now. I had a thing for boys even before my pubertal hormones started raging. I just wanted to get next to them; I had no clear idea why. As a teenager, I began to think I knew why, and it had something to do with their bodies, which were very intriguing. This thing for guys hasn't let up since. I wouldn't say I'm the straightest arrow in the quiver, but I have a fairly established sexual preference, and it's hetero. For years after college, during which I read and adopted a lot of the prevailing wisdom about the "polymorphous perversity" of the unsocialized human individual, I walked around in the belief that I, like everyone else, was fundamentally bisexual. I figured there were some people with stronger tendencies in one direction or the other, but that I was more or less in the middle, ready to ride the winds of social acceptability wherever they blew me. I was trained to find males attractive, to fall in love with them, and ultimately to find a nice man with whom to settle down and have children. And I did just that. But, I reasoned, if I had been raised in a culture that smiled on exclusive homosexuality alone, I would have found a nice woman, fallen in love with her, and we would have settled down together to raise a family.

In recent years I've come to doubt that. I've seen too many basically conformist, don't-rock-the-boat-type friends embark on secret careers of homosexuality. If they were willing to brave this forbidden terrain, they with all their desire to appear "normal" (and sometimes even with a deep conviction that they were angering God and endangering their eventual salvation by engaging in homosexual acts), then something pretty strong, pretty convention-defying, must be driving them. I've come to suspect that my heterosexuality is more like this. Yes, if I'd been raised in a homophilic culture, I probably would have fallen in love with a woman and settled down with her to raise a family. And on my way home from work, I'd be stopping off at the hetero porn shop to peek at pictures of naked men. Maybe one night while the wife and kids were visiting her parents, I'd head for the local straight bar, telling myself it was a sociological sort of interest, not a personal one ... that I just wanted to take a look, the better to explain sexual perversions to my gender studies students, you understand. But it would only be a question of time before I'd be kissing my wife good-bye on our front porch, saying "sorry, sweetie, you know I don't *want* to go out of town this weekend, but business demands it," and then I'd be slipping into the car, putting on my hat and dark glasses, and driving two and a half miles to a sleazy hotel where I would check into my room and wait for my secret lover, a—gasp!—*man*.

Again, I'm not suggesting that homosexual desire is linked to being more or less feminine or more or less manly. But people who step outside society's favored sexual preference tend to run afoul of its ideas about gender, and are therefore often forced to question their gender identity more deeply. I haven't had that pressure. Indeed, right now I live in one of the more sex-defined, heterosexist American subcultures you can imagine. At least 90 percent of my social life (such as it is) is spent with other heterosexual couples and their (and our) children. We're all at least quasi feminists, having come of age during an era when women and men could be friends and not just lovers, so at parties we make a point of speaking with members of the other sex. It's a farce though. It's never more than fifteen minutes before the women are all huddled in the kitchen together while the guys are out back stoking the grill. I've listened in on these male conversations by the barbecue. As often as not, they're talking about their children, just as we are: how to stop little Hannah from pitching fits in the grocery store, what's causing Alex's sleep problems, where Kayla should go for summer camp. But we do this in different rooms as often as politely possible. We women watch to make sure that the men occasionally prepare a salad or set the table, that they change diapers and wipe noses and go check on the kids when we hear screams from upstairs. But when someone gets in the car to go buy a six-pack, it's always someone with a penis.

I do all right in this universe. And yet the occasions on which femaleness has felt to me like a sweet smooth body stocking are easily outnumbered by those times when it's been like a suit of clothes that itches and rubs and pulls and just doesn't feel right.

There are degrees of discomfort, obviously. I would not undergo surgery and hormone treatments to become a man. Even if a genie appeared and promised to make me a man with no knives, no drugs, and no scarring, I'd turn down the offer flat. I've invested a lot of work in being a woman. Why would I want to be a man? Oh, I can see that there are advantages. Even if you think that on balance women have it just as good as men, even if the word *patriarchy* would never trip off your tongue, you'd have to admit that there are perks associated with being equipped with one penis, one Y chromosome, and a whole host of androgens—things you can do more easily and with less social disapprobation if you're a man. But the way I look at it, I'd be trading in one set of itchy clothes for another. What's the profit in that?

So call me a relatively well adjusted heterosexual individual with two X chromosomes, a standard-issue set of external and internal female organs, apparently normal hormone levels, and a comparatively fixed sense of herself as a woman (that is to say, a gender identity that I don't particularly want to disrupt).

And yet I've always suspected that there's something not-all-there about my femaleness. Not something—many things. Appearances notwithstanding, my femaleness has never felt unquestioned to me even on that level that people like to call "the obvious biological sex differences."

For example, from the time I was a teenager, I wondered if my vulva really was like other women's, or if it somehow betrayed my not-all-thereness as a woman. Was my clitoris bigger? Did I have more pubic hair? Did I smell the same, taste the same, feel the same as other women? I confided this to a friend recently. I asked her if she'd ever worried about that sort of thing when she was younger. "Of course not!" she exclaimed. "Didn't you ever look at a *Playboy* magazine?" she asked. I did. I know I did. (And recall, this was during the era when the split-beaver shot had become de rigeur in *Playboy*.) But a two-dimensional photograph can only tell you so much. I wanted to know about the rest. Like my vagina didn't feel at all like I thought a vagina should feel. It was kind of folded in on itself in a funky way. I imagined that if you could shine a light in there, it would look like brain coral. I had thought my vagina would be constructed on analogy with other bodily orifices: like a nostril, with its definite interior shape, its moistness, its smoothness. My vagina was not like that. It was moist, but kind of shapeless and lumpy. For my first ten or so pelvic exams, I kept waiting for the gynecologist to comment on some peculiarity of my genitalia. "Did you know your vagina is extremely foreshortened?" he might say, or maybe "Whew, you're a hairy little beast, aren't you?" or maybe "Ye gods, look at the size of those labia! You don't mind if I call in my colleague, Dr. Jones, do you? I want him to see this. Fascinating, absolutely fascinating." I had a different gynecologist every year, between school health centers and Planned Parenthood clinics and HMOs. None of them ever said anything like that. I came to assume that I must be somewhere in the normal range in the vagina department.

This didn't stop me from submitting every long-term lover to a pop quiz about the characteristics of my vulva vis-à-vis those of other women's. After all, they'd done field research, and I hadn't; their information base was substantially larger. Men are reputed to be very rational and logical. They're supposed to tromp all over your delicate feelings about personal matters with blithe indifference when a matter of natural fact is at stake. But every man I asked gave the same basic answer, a beautiful multi-faceted gem of nuanced diplomacy. In every particular, they assured me, my enchilada was as other women's. Neither particularly large nor small, hairy nor sparse, wet nor dry, and so on. However, they added, for all that similarity, there was something extra special about mine; it had some ineffable charm that others lacked.

I didn't flat out believe them. I'm not that stupid. Men eager for a good game of hide-the-salami will say just about whatever they think you want to hear. But at some point, the preponderance of evidence has led me to believe that my not-all-thereness as a woman cannot be detected in the physical contours of my vagina.

So I located it elsewhere. A favorite place has long been my body hair. Women have body hair. Lots of it. In fact, here's a news flash: *women grow hair everywhere that men do.* It is sometimes paler, finer, and less plentiful than the hair of men, but this usually has more to do with race and ethnicity than with sex (for example, a Slavic woman is likely to be hairier than a Chinese man). I was never a pathbreaker when it came to feminine rites of passage. Pantyhose and training bras and fingernail polish were things I only came to well after the bulk of my peers had adopted them. When I did adopt them, it was more because I wanted to fit in than because I had any independent interest in strapping elastic around my chest or hauling nylon stockings up my legs or shellacking my fingernails. But boy did I ever want to shave my legs. I lobbied for permission to do so before I left elementary school, and it was eventually granted. I managed to hack up my flesh pretty thoroughly, but I never for a moment questioned the worthwhileness of this enterprise. I had found a way to hide my secret shame: a perfectly acceptable, very grown-up way of hiding my secret shame. What could be better?

I shaved my armpits too. Once I had the technology, I used it just about everywhere. No sooner did I begin to grow pubic hair than I began to shave it off (just the "bikini line," you understand), leaving pimply red welts in two lovely strips along my upper thighs. There were stray hairs on my stomach. These, I found, could be shaved as well, as could the hair on my elbows and toes. When my friend Janet handed me a pair of tweezers, suggesting that I might want to thin out the turf along my brow ridge, I embraced that technology as well. There were three dark hairs growing between my breasts. Yank! Gone. There was a long black hair growing out of a mole on my arm. Yank! Gone. If you didn't know any better, you'd have thought I was a real woman.

I did know better though. And I was convinced that all that body hair spoke of some subterranean maleness that my chromosomes and genitalia had cleverly eluded, but that was nevertheless there in every last hair follicle on my body. I could fool the world (after all, everybody else was shaving their legs and armpits too), but I knew that shaving was no once-a-week spot-check operation with me. It was a daily all-body ritual.

By the time I was in college, I began to sprout chin hairs. I'd seen plenty of movies by this point in my life, and I knew that men liked to take their big broad hands and lift up your silky chin so they could plant a wet one on your soft sweet lips. I became adept at avoiding this maneuver. (I'll tell you the trick: when they start to reach for your chin, grab their hand and stick it on the closest available breast. Singularly effective.) I policed my chin every morning, and yet there were many times when I'd glance in the rearview mirror of my car only to find a big black porcupine quill sticking out of my face. "How could I have missed that?" I would panic, while dipping into my purse for my spare pair of tweezers, sometimes not even waiting for a red light to execute the necessary plucking operation.

But then in my early twenties I decided on an impulse to grow out my leg and armpit hair. The direct inspiration for this was my German-American roommate, Lise, who had never taken a razor to her flesh, not anywhere. She thought it was a sicko American thing, this shaving obsession. I thought Lise's hairy legs, especially under a pair of nylon stockings with all the little hairs being dragged this way and that, were nothing short of disgusting. I couldn't imagine why any woman living in America, with easy access to a razor and soap, would walk around looking like that. And yet I grew my own leg hair out that winter (you didn't think I was going to do it in the middle of the summer, did you?) in solidarity with Lise. At the time, I told myself that it was strictly a matter of curiosity, that I had been shaving at least every other day for more than ten years, and I wanted to see exactly what I was shaving off.

Let me tell you, all that hair was gross. I immediately wanted to shave again, but I didn't feel like I could while Lise was living with me. It would have seemed too much like a slap in her face, since we had had long heartfelt discussions about the misogynistic implications of American women shaving their legs. But the morning I put Lise on a Greyhound bus to Nevada, I went straight home, popped in a fresh blade, and rendered myself hair-free. I felt like a woman again.

Except that I didn't, not really. Because I knew that I was faking it, that I couldn't manage an acceptable level of bodily femaleness without artificial help from my razor and my tweezers. I think that's what drove me to grow it all out again a little over a year later. I wanted to let my body go its hairy way and convince myself that I was plenty female like that, just the way God made me. I saw this as a bold, reverse-psychological counterattack. "Yes, you're hairy," I imagined my armpits saying to the rest of me. "So what? You're still all woman."

In the midst of this experiment with in-your-face hairy femaleness, I took a camping trip through western Canada by myself. I thought it was a very independent, free spirit sort of thing to do, but it only took a few days for terminal boredom to set in. When at a hostel in Banff I met up with a German guy who was hitchhiking his way across Canada, we quickly figured out that if we teamed up we would both have access to his tent (much nicer than mine), my car (better than his thumb), and each other's company. And so we spent a week or so camping and hiking together.

My legs and armpits were at about a quarter of an inch at this point, and growing. Around five days into our vacation we stopped for lunch at a beautifully crystalline lake in Mount Robson Park in British Columbia. We took off our hiking boots and waded into the frigid water.

"Is it true that all women in America shave their legs?" Michael asked me.

"Pretty much," I said.

"And under the axis too?" he inquired, gesturing under his arms.

"Yup," I replied.

"Hmmmpff," Michael grunted. "That's stupid. Women don't do that in Germany. It's a very foolish American custom."

"I know," I said, glad to finally be on the correct side of a cross-cultural dispute. "I just stopped shaving a couple of weeks ago," I pointed out to him. "You can see that mine is growing in."

"Yes, I noticed," Michael said. "Your legs are very hairy. Even in Germany I think you would have to shave."

Glitches like this notwithstanding, no man has ever declined to get naked with me solely because of my hairy legs and armpits. More significantly perhaps, no man—friend or lover—has declined to be seen in public with me, even when I was wearing shorts and a tank top (which requires a bit more bravery on his part, I think you'll agree). Most summers I've gone ahead and shaved my legs, but I haven't shaved my armpits for nearly a decade. I like my armpits this way. Really. Yes, there's a bit of a feminist political statement at work here. But it's just as much a matter of aesthetic preference. I've always liked men's hairy armpits, and now I have my own.

Not that I never experience any ambivalence on this matter. Last week, on the first fine spring day of the year, I was carrying Lucy, my nine-month-old baby, into her day care center. She was in her car seat, balanced on my hip, and we were both in our summer clothes for the first time since early last fall. With that look of intent curiosity that she wears on her face whenever anything unprecedented appears (a common event in her life at this stage), she reached up and grabbed a few armpit hairs in a pincer grip with her tiny fingers. She looked puzzled. She twisted them a bit. She broke into a huge grin. Then she laughed out loud.

"Oh Jesus," I thought, unable to disengage her fingers because I didn't have a free hand, "please don't let any of the other parents see this." I wondered again if I shouldn't just cave in and make like a normal woman. It wouldn't take more than sixty seconds every couple of days to shave my armpits. I could play with my husband's armpit hair if I got the urge, I reasoned to myself; I didn't need any of my own.

Am I a woman then? Of course, but ... but what? Well, maybe I could be a woman who's slightly off hormonally, a somewhat mannish woman. I read an article several years ago about women with higher-than-normal (for women) testosterone levels. These women were more aggressive than other women, they were more interested in sex, they were less likely to be married and have children and more likely to have successful careers. I unpacked that chunk of rhetoric in no time. Come on, I make no bones about it: I'm a feminist. Not the sweet, reasonable kind; the pissy, bad-tempered kind. "What bullshit!" I hollered in my empty office, tossing the magazine to the floor, fuming. Then I picked it up again so I could read the sidebar listing the signs of too much testosterone in women. "Maybe this is why I'm not like other women," I mused to myself. "Maybe I have an excess of testosterone." There it all was: facial hair, high energy, loves sex, savors achievement. . . .

This might make it easier to explain why a double-X-chromosome-bearing, vulva-owning, menstruating, baby-birthing, lactating heterosexual suburban mother-of-two has often felt her femaleness to be an itchy, annoying, not-all-there sort of thing. Except that I had my testosterone checked not long after that. Not because of the article. Well ... not directly. I was having my hormone levels tested to see if there was anything out of whack that might be contributing to my severe PMS. I really only needed to test my progesterone and my estrogen for that, but I told them to check my testosterone too, as long as they were at it. It turned out everything was in the normal range, except my testosterone. I had the testosterone level of a seventy-five-year-old woman. The lab recommended that I speak with my doctor about prescribing testosterone supplements to help me cope with the effects of my hormonal deficiency: you know, hair loss, lethargy, low sex drive ... that kind of thing.

Physiologically speaking, then, am I woman, when you put it all together? Yes, I imagine so, in spite of my neurotic worries over the years. Still, I can't say that I'm happy with any of the definitions of physiological femaleness (or maleness) that I've considered here. There are people I would want to call women who don't menstruate or who have no breasts or who couldn't pass a chromosome test for female Olympic athletes. And I'm not sure that a person with XY chromosomes who has lived thirty years as a man and now has a surgically constructed vagina is a woman. I'm not sure she's not. It just seems to me that the nature of biological sex is vastly more complicated and poorly understood than we typically surmise, that it's not so all-or-nothing, male-or-female, as people make it out to be.

There are clearly some physiological traits that go toward constituting femaleness. But it's also obvious that someone is loading the dice pretty seriously. For example, women on average have larger breasts than men, so men aren't supposed to have any breasts at all. I saw a television news magazine segment on this a few weeks ago. It emphasized the great trauma suffered by men who have observable breast tissue (sometimes as much as a B cup!). There's nothing detectably "wrong" with these men, no hormone imbalance or extra chromosome. They just have breasts. Gynecomastia, it's called: breasts like a woman's. The television commentator suggested that simple human charity should dictate surgical redress for these men. No man should have to go through life with breasts.

Or in an example closer to my heart, men are on average hairier than women, so women shouldn't be hairy at all. I talked to my electrologist, Eileen, about this one day. (You can tell I haven't completely overcome my fetish for eradicating telltale unfeminine body hair.) She told me that lots of her clients are positively mortified when they first come in. "They all think they're the hairiest thing that ever lived," she says. "They'll sit down and ask nervously, 'Have you ever seen anything like this before?'" (I remembered asking her this very question some eight or nine years ago, sitting in that very same chair. I didn't remind her of this.) I asked Eileen what proportion of the female population she thought had facial hair, conspicuous facial hair. "Oh, ninety percent," she answered confidently. "Everyone is waxing or bleaching or tweezing if they're not getting electrolysis."

"The funny thing is," she said thoughtfully, "being worried about your body hair doesn't have anything to do with how much you have. I get women in here who look like the missing link, and all they want done is their fingers or something like that. And then, like I had a woman in here the other day who couldn't have had more than six strands of facial hair, I swear, all of them blond. I could barely see them, even under the magnifier. But she was absolutely freaking out. She told me that she'd already been to her doctor's office, insisting that something must be medically wrong with her to have these six hairs on her face.

"Lots of women treat it like a total secret," she went on. "They tell me, 'Here's my office number; don't ever call me at home, because my husband doesn't know about this.' Or they say, 'If you call and my husband answers, tell him you're calling from the nail salon, okay?' I had one woman in here a couple of months ago. She was an actress, absolutely stunning. She was waiting to put together a portfolio until after the electrolysis was done, until 'I get this fixed,' she said. I told her how gorgeous she was, and that she shouldn't let a few facial hairs slow her down, and she said 'I can't help it, I just hate it. I'm such a *man*.'"

Let's say my electrologist overestimated. She's a professional hair remover; she'd be bound to overestimate, don't you think? So how about if we say that only 60 percent of North American women have significant facial hair? Now I would submit that any characteristic exhibited by 60 percent of women is by definition not a "masculine" trait. So why do we treat it as though it were? As though nature had made some horrible mistakes, and that if we didn't fix them by surgically removing men's breasts and electrically frying women's facial hair follicles, then the two sexes might just slide right on into each other? That they might —perish the thought—become indistinct?

That is, why is it that we're so inordinately eager to polarize the two most common biological sexes (not the only ones, remember) ever further than "nature" alone would dictate? If as physical, sexed beings we are more alike than we at first seem, what's going on here that could account for such exaggerations?

In fairness, I think we have to consider whether or not there are other, more important markers of femaleness and maleness apart from physiology. Maybe they justify the classificatory separation we demand between women and men and exaggerate via practices like cosmetic surgery or electrolysis. Perhaps our emotional lives are strikingly differentiated by sex, even though our bodies betray a good deal of similarity. Maybe our brains are wired differently, such that our experience of the world is dramatically different. Or maybe the experience of being born of women rather than men produces entirely different psychological centers of gravity in men's and women's psyches. What does it feel like to be a woman? What does a woman feel like?

CHAPTER 3

Feeling for Others: Women and Emotion

I've already admitted that I feel like a woman only intermittently and unpredictably, so maybe I'm not the right person to say what femaleness feels like. But I'll take a crack at it anyway. If I can't say exactly what it is to feel like a woman, I do know some things it *isn't*. Like it can't be primarily about any of the physiological things we've discussed. Does getting my period make me feel like a woman? Well, it doesn't make me feel like a *man*. But some people—for example, women past menopause or after a hysterectomy—presumably feel like women without menstruating. Indeed, some transvestites and transsexuals say that they feel like women without benefit of menstruating, having a vagina or breasts, or even the donning of women's clothing. They say they feel like women all the time, down deep, regardless of how they're dressed or which bathroom they're using.

So what is this sense of femaleness, this peculiar characteristic (or set of characteristics) that can be experienced by individuals with a penis and XY chromosomes, and not experienced by individuals with a vagina and XX chromosomes, but is nevertheless "female"? What does it consist of?

Maybe it's simply a matter of slipping into femaleness (whether by nature or intervention) and finding oneself comfy and at home there. It's the opposite, in other words, of experiencing femaleness as an itchy, annoying suit of clothes. But I'm guessing it has something to do with feelings. Not just "feeling like a woman," but having the feelings that women are supposed to have.

Quantity is important here, I think. Yes, there are definite feelings women are supposed to have, but we're also supposed to have a lot of feelings, period. I've been on a Thomas Hardy kick lately. A friend lent me several books of Hardy's on tape, and as I drive from work to day care to home, some very British actor natters on and on about the nineteenth-century English countryside and the quaint doings there. Now if Hardy cares about two things, they're sex and religion (which is possibly why I find him so entertaining). And from *Tess of the D'Urbervilles* to *The Mayor of Casterbridge,* Hardy is noteworthy for his sympathetic portrayals of women and the terrible situations they're forced into by nineteenth-century English custom (read: sexism). The man was a regular protofeminist. When he wasn't being a chauvinist creep, that is. For Hardy knows that men are men and women are women, and if you chew through enough of his novels, it's easy to tell the difference between them. Women are the people who have big, frequent emotions that they act on in spite of themselves, even when this leads them into disaster (as it almost always does). They are tragic figures. Men are also tragic, but in a different way: their passions sometimes trip them up, but just as often it is their intellects that deceive them. Think of Angel Clare, so committed to his philosophical views regarding the moral purity of the English farm folk that at great pain to himself he leaves Tess Darbyfield, the love of his life, rather than reconsider the conclusions to which his intellect has brought him.

If you don't trust Thomas Hardy on this, then spend a little time on the Internet. Surf on over to www.thespark.com, where you can get the answer to that pesky question "are you a man or a woman?" for a lot less time and energy than it will take you to read this. Not only will you save time, but the test is "super-scientific" and "remarkably accurate" (claims I do not make here). These folks state that without "asking about your clothes, grooming, or penis" (that is, you can skip most of what I've written thus far), they can "predict, with 100 percent accuracy, whether you're a guy or a girl."

This test has fifty questions. I've taken it four times. The first time, I answered as truthfully as I could. That was three months ago. I couldn't answer *perfectly* truthfully; there were two or three questions where I was genuinely torn between the answers they offered. In those cases I chose what I thought was probably the guy answer. Because that's just the sort of person I am. When I sent my completed answer sheet off through cyberspace, the verdict returned almost instantly: I was a guy. If you believe their claims about 100 percent accuracy, then I can quit writing right now. Am I a woman? Apparently not. But then I took the test again today to see if I really could tell which were the guy answers and which the girl answers, as I suspected I could. Answering as a man, to the best of my ability, I was a man, at a 93 percent confidence level (which was way better than my initial verdict as a guy, around 60 percent certainty). Answering as a woman, again to the best of my ability, I was a woman, at an 86 percent confidence level. Finally, I tried again to answer the test honestly, as myself. By then I'd already blown the whole point of it by trying to ferret out the secret meanings of these seemingly innocuous questions. However, on the last go-around I was a woman, at an 80 percent confidence level. Whew. What this proves, I believe, is that all pretense aside, I want to be a woman and am willing to do whatever I have to by way of self-deception to seem like one, even if the only one looking at the verdict is myself.

Of course, the Spark's claims about 100 percent accuracy are retarded. One of the questions, number 21, refers to this specifically: "Our claim that we can guess everyone's gender is 'impressive' and yet 'retarded,' writes one Spark fan. Which is it?" Believe me, the only time I clicked "impressive" was when I was really, really trying to be a woman.

The good folks at thespark.com ask all sorts of questions on their test, but many of them fit into the broad category of woman=emotion, man=intellect. (Or, formulated another way, woman=people, man=things.) Here are some examples: "Do you ever think about the beginning of time and wish you could've been there to witness it?" Clearly the guy answer is yes, and the girl answer is no. It's intellectual curiosity versus "but I'd be all alone!" Or this one: "Do you think that one day there will be world peace?" Well, if you're a hazy feel-good type (i.e., a woman) you say yes, whereas if you're a hardheaded realist (i.e., a man) you say no. Some questions are rather obscure. One asks you to finish a sequence of five squares and circles. Neither answer they provide is optimal. You can either end with a circle of an inappropriate color, or with the right color, but in the shape of a triangle. What does this have to do with gender? I'm guessing that girls like pretty colors. Guys like a logical progression of formal shape. Other questions are much more transparent. "Technology always prevails: True or false?" Duh. Don't need that gender studies Ph.D. to know how to answer that one. Or "What is the greater value of the Internet? Information or communication?" At this point, I began to think they might just as well have a one-question test: "Do you prefer to think of yourself as a man or a woman?"

Some women prefer to think of themselves as men. For example, I know a woman who was out on a first date with a guy who was trying hard to impress her with how spectacularly attractive she was to him. He told her she was perfect. He said she was "like a guy, only with breasts." She found this very amusing, and she thought this definition suited her very well. She took on the acronym GWB ("guy with breasts") for her email signature line, and whenever she didn't react to life's little trials as people thought she should, she would exclaim, "What can I say? I'm a guy with breasts."

It's interesting to note what situations caused her to cite her essential GWBiness in order to explain her peculiar—for a woman—reactions. They were situations where she would be expected to exhibit deep and painful emotion, but didn't. Like when she broke up with a longtime boyfriend and just got on with it, not pausing to have a nervous breakdown or to sit all night in her car outside his apartment with a box of Kleenex on the passenger seat or even to spend an evening seeking consolation in a pint of chocolate ice cream and a bag of pretzels.

I don't want to waste time quibbling over this, but anyone who has lived through their teens and twenties knows that your average guy will react to a breakup by holing up in his apartment, giving up on personal hygiene, and extrapolating from this one unfortunate relationship to the rather drastic conclusion that all women are bitches (or something like that). This does not qualify as breezy indifference, or even calm, reasoned resignation.

But let's bypass these irritating counterexamples and get back to the heart of the matter. Am I a woman? If being emotional makes you a woman, I'm a veritable drag queen, a woman so very womanly as to very nearly qualify as a joke. Unmedicated anyway, I can cry over anything. Indeed, I can cry over absolutely nothing. With gusto.

I would glory over being unquestionably female this way, except that even here I detect telltale signs of masculinity. Because being a woman is not so simple as having big noisy feelings. Women are believed to be intuitive: they are supposed to trust in their feelings more than they believe in their thoughts. A woman, it is thought, will always choose a moment of sweet rapport with another human being over a stubborn opinion, a relationship over a fact. For me, stubborn opinions and an attachment to facts are the coarse chin hairs on my weepy feminine personality. As for being intuitive, well, I'll take a compliment anywhere I can find it, but anyone who knows me would have to say I'm far more prone to doggedly linear progressions of logic. A Socratic dialogue is always playing somewhere in the back of my mind even in the midst of a crying jag over something ridiculous. "Waaah, waaah," I will be moaning, and inside I'll be thinking, "How curious! What could be the source of this anguish? Is it disproportionate to the identified stimulus? Are there other proximate factors to consider?" "If P then Q," my mind drones on, day in and day out, in the binary true/false rea-

soning of computers and, supposedly, men. Big emotions notwithstanding then, maybe I am a GWB, a guy with breasts.

Even some feminist acquaintances have concurred in this
assessment of me. They don't say I'm a GWB; they say I'm a
"male-identified woman." It's a similar epithet, except in the
latter case you are not only like a man, but you are (either
subconsciously or deliberately) selling out all your sisters in a
pathetic grab for approval and success on male terms. As a male-
identified woman, they say, I am not being true to my authentic
female self when I reason in the binary fashion that I experience
as second nature. I am merely mimicking the phallogocentrism
of patriarchal culture.

Phallogocentrism: now that's a mouthful. The term was
coined by French feminist Hélène Cixous. It is a spin on psychoanalyst Jacques Lacan's concept of phallocentrism (the cen-
trality of men and their phallic genital equipment), with the
inclusion of the Greek word *logos*—words, speech, language,
discourse—at its center. Why "logos"? Because speech, in the
thinking of Cixous and the psychoanalysts on whom she draws,
is born out of the Oedpial drama. The same process that centers "the phallus" in the life of little boys (and from there,
grown men and human culture as a whole) gives rise to language. Language is, in this form of reasoning, phallic. Hence,
"phallogocentrism."

The first basis for this theory is the Freudian idea that the infant does not distinguish himself (and I use the male pronoun
advisedly here) from his mother, that he perceives no separation
between him and her but instead feels a blissful continuity of
warm, loving body that is himself/mother. The boy only gradually comes to understand that he has his own body and that it
is not coterminous with his mother's. All develops smoothly in
this way until he encounters the real crisis, the one that will forever separate him from his mother: his discovery that their genitals do not match. He is a boy; he has a penis. She is a not-boy,
a person without a penis. (According to Freud, the little boy initially perceives her as a castrated man, as someone whose penis

has been taken away from her.) This is the Oedipal crisis, which, if all goes as it should, is resolved when the boy comes to identify with his father, to perceive himself as one who will grow to be a man.

Many post-Freudians, especially feminists, have felt that Freud did not pay enough attention to the first stage he postulated: the symbiotic, mother-centered, pre-Oedipal stage. Freud was eager to get on to the excitement of the Oedipal drama and did not dwell heavily on the immersion-in-the-feminine, the merger-with-the-mother that was simply its precursor. (This tendency to magnify the trauma of becoming male is a consistent feature of Freud's thought.) Others, coming after Freud, have wanted to insist that the pre-Oedipal experience of merger is as significant in adults' lives as the Oedipal crisis, that both these stages live on as psychological realities that influence adult feeling and behavior from their shadowed homes in the subconscious.

One such post-Freudian psychoanalyst is the aforementioned French theorist Jacques Lacan. Lacan is noteworthy for, among other things, equating the Oedipal crisis with the acquisition of language and the pre-Oedipal stage with its absence. He says that what the little boy does to identify with his father is something more subtle and complex—and ultimately more significant for the way the world is structured—than desiring his mother sexually, fearing castration from his father, and finally coming to think of himself as male as a self-protective move, a way to hang on to that little penis. What Lacanian little boys do is to "enter into language," to depend on language's "symbolic order" to establish their manliness over against their mother's bodily, cuddly, nonverbal connection with them as infants. As Cixous (among others) has noted, just as males and females, self and (m)other, come to be opposed in the boy's thinking, so is language itself—and therefore, to some degree, thought—structured around a series of binary oppositions like order/chaos, presence/absence, good/evil. In all cases, the first term is more valuable and is associated with the male, and the second term is inferior and associated with the female. Phallogocentrism.

How do girls fit into all this? Poorly. Girls don't have to break away from their mothers; they just take a bath together in their shared female embodiedness and keep right on cuddling into advanced middle age. Oh, girls learn to *talk* all right, but it's a sideways step for them, one that is never as fully incorporated into their identities as it is for little boys. Women forever exist at a remove from language, which is basically a male invention. They are, in Lacanian terms, "on the edge of the Symbolic," while men—or "the phallus," if you prefer—are at its center.

You can see how easy it is to be male-identified in a setup like this. Although Cixous is eager to mark out a special, subversive place for women in this scheme—using language to express the prelinguistic (that can't be easy) through *l'écriture feminine*—it's tough not to sound like a man if you're talking in full sentences and employing prepositional phrases. Well, just give me my penis right now. I can't imagine thinking in another way, and I'm hard pressed to understand why I would want to. (Except perhaps for my fledgling desire to be counted as a woman, a real woman.)

The other suspicious note of masculinity in my feelings is this: While I can work up a good cry over, say, a touching story, I'm most inclined to deep emotion in relation to my own life. Women's emotionality, as I understand it, includes this source of angst, but its true hallmark is the ability to feel not only for oneself but for others. I mean, men are permitted emotion too. Anger is generally thought more suitable than sadness for masculine purposes, but emotion is emotion, and in regard to the mishaps of their own lives, men are expected to react from their hearts as well as their heads. If you're a man, for example, you can blow your stack over a minor traffic incident, and no one will take this irrationality as a sign of your latent femininity. But men are supposed to suffer from a stolid lack of affect when it comes to the miseries of others. The classic male approach to other people's emotions is thought to be cold-blooded analysis. If a feeling doesn't make sense, it can safely be ignored as so much static. Certainly it should not be the object of sympathetic understanding.

Women, on the other hand, are supposed to feel and feel and feel for others, to be a veritable sink of empathy. At least this is how I learned femaleness. "Being a good listener" and "not being selfish" were among the few absolutely explicit instructions in femininity that I got from my mother.

There were idiosyncratic factors at work here. My mother was the youngest in a large family with a dictatorial father and a martyred mother. She made the obvious choice between role models. She would be patient and kind like her mother, not arbitrary and cruel like her father. But at the same time, my mother's views fit into a larger model of female selflessness (contrasted with male self-assertion) that is still very easy to come by culturally—for example, at the movies.

Recently, at a friend's insistence, I rented the film *What Women Want* with Mel Gibson and Helen Hunt. If you haven't seen it, here is the basic setup: Nick (Mel Gibson) is an advertising executive who is passed over for a promotion that is filled from the outside by Darcy (Helen Hunt). The agency knows it must sell products targeted for women, and they feel they need a feminine sensibility that cannot be provided by chauvinistic Nick—a divorced father of a teenaged daughter. Responding to a challenge from his new boss, Darcy, Nick sullenly goes home and experiments with the various products the agency needs to advertise: lipstick, fingernail polish, control-top pantyhose, leg wax, mascara, a hair dryer, and so forth. He has a mishap in the bathtub, gets fried by the hair dryer, and zap! . . .he is suddenly able to hear what women are thinking. Their inner monologues are audible inside his very own head.

Panicked, Nick goes to a therapist he hasn't seen for years (Bette Midler). She quickly sizes up the situation and advises him, "If men are from Mars and women are from Venus and you speak Venusian, the world is yours!" Nick sees the wisdom in this and promptly sets out to use his new insight into women to ruin Darcy's career so that he can get the promotion he feels he deserved in the first place.

While listening in on their thoughts, Nick gets a reputation among the women at work for being sensitive and understanding. He is also able to come up with dynamite ad campaigns that seemingly magically speak to women's deepest moods and feelings. Of course, this is Hollywood, and although Nick is able to achieve his goal of getting Darcy fired and himself ensconced in her position, his goal turns out not to have been a worthy one. Nick learns a Life Lesson. Having set out to use his strange ability to prevail over women, Nick acquires instead a newfound ability to identify with women and their concerns. Toward the end of the movie, Nick rescues a female coworker who is on the brink of suicide and offers her a job; he tracks down Darcy and promises to get her job back for her; he finds his daughter (who is at her high school prom) and comforts her after her boyfriend dumps her for refusing to have sex with him. "Believe it or not," Nick tells his daughter, "I know what it's like to be a woman, and it's not as easy as it looks."

What does Nick mean? What's hard about being a woman? Well, first there is the incredible pain women suffer for the sake of beauty, something we see graphically illustrated as Nick tries to rip out his leg hair with wax and darken his eyelashes with mascara. But we'll come to that later. What he learns more profoundly is how women feel: "They worry about everything all the time," Nick tells a friend. And they suffer suffer suffer at the hands of men, who are terminally insensitive. After this brief glimpse into how the other half feels, Nick experiences the full shame of having ruined Darcy's career. (By this time he is romantically involved with her.) He muses, "A woman wouldn't have screwed over the woman she loved. They don't think that way." Then, in a bow to Doctor Freud, Nick asserts to a male friend, "You know who has penis envy? We do. That's why we cheat and screw up and lie. Because we're all obsessed with our own equipment, that's why."

What do we learn about gender in this movie? Quite simply that women are good and loving and kind, and that men are assholes who can't see past the end of their own dicks. Well . . . men aren't total assholes. They can improve; they can learn from their mistakes; they can grow up. But they don't start out compassionate and nurturing the way women do. They start out thinking only of themselves and have to be brought around, to the degree that they can be, by the women in their lives.

This is the model I grew up with. I heard it at home, I read it in books, I watched it on television. And I wanted to be a good woman, the right kind of woman, a woman who thought of others before herself all the time. (This preoccupation with selflessness was exacerbated by the fact that we were Christians, exhorted to imitate Jesus in all that we did. Since Jesus was reportedly thinking of others all the time and was willing to suffer a painful death for his friends—for all of us—this was quite a high standard to uphold.) Yet, as my mother was quick to inform me, I was not on the road to becoming a good woman, because I was selfish. For years I struggled mightily to be more giving and forgiving, more concerned about the feelings of others, less wrapped up in my own dreary little concerns.

This drama reached its peak when I was in graduate school, trying halfheartedly to be a Zen Buddhist. The Buddhist idea that the self was an illusion was one I knew absolutely to be true the first time I heard it. I didn't need any koans or vipassana meditation to understand that the habit of thinking of oneself, of valuing oneself as an ongoing entity, was wrong, especially for a woman. But now here was a technique that I could consciously manipulate to turn myself into the person I knew I was supposed to be, a person who was filled with compassion for others while constantly holding the clear comprehension of the complete emptiness of herself.

So I set out to meditate. Actually, I had a very hard time sitting still, so I tried a shortcut: I would walk around living my

ordinary life, but I would watch my thoughts at the same time
(which is what you were supposed to do while meditating:
watch your thoughts rise up and fall away, and realize that you
are not your thoughts).

I guess I expected that my thought-watching would reveal
that I was dwelling rather heavily on the fiction of my continuing selfhood, since that was its stated goal. But I was astounded
at just how bad it really was. I thought about myself *all the time.*
I invented imaginary dialogues between myself and others, in
which I was always sounding very clever. I spent literal hours
of mental time figuring out how to satisfy my desires, from
big questions like whether or not I should stay in graduate
school to tiny ones like what flavor of ice cream I should buy at
the grocery store on my way home. Also, as I watched my
thoughts, I noticed that certain ones were conspicuously absent
from my unguarded inner monologue. I did not think about the
sufferings of the oppressed in Nicaragua and what I, as a first-
world person of privilege, could do to help them. The nuclear
arms race, which figured prominently in my academic thinking
and political organizing at the time, was a cipher. Pffft, who
cared? I didn't even bother to think about my friends and family and their problems all that often, so consumed was I in my
own. Only very rarely—okay, maybe once, and probably while
stoned—did I take a look at my thoughts and perceive that I was
emptying myself out so that I could be a bodhisattva, continuing to exist only out of compassion for others.

I really believed in this Buddhist stuff; I desperately wanted
to do it right. At that point I had been trying for nearly two
decades to learn this hard lesson in selflessness, and I was very
much hoping that I could finally get it right. But instead, I gave
up trying. At 3:30 in the morning, to be exact. I had stayed
awake for about forty hours drinking endless cups of coffee,
grading student papers, and reading about phenomenological
theory. Not a bright thing to do, certainly, but very much a
part of the graduate student ethos. I finally collapsed in bed at
midnight, still on a wicked caffeine buzz, and had bizarre night-

mares followed by the jolting waking conviction a few hours later that I was so selfish, so totally wrapped up in this illusion of self, that it would be quicker to kill myself than to spend years in meditation trying to get past it. Suicide seemed the more obvious, culturally appropriate place to go with intense self-loathing anyway. We are not Buddhists in America. We are aficionados of firearms. Go back to your roots, I told myself, bow to your ancestors who pioneered the American West. Blam! Put an end to it.

I didn't kill myself. In the back of my mind, I knew that what I really needed was a good night's sleep, a large, nourishing breakfast, and a good talking to. I started with the last. I called my sister, and she drove over to my apartment in the middle of the night. She told me over and over again that she could not care less if Zen Buddhists were absolutely right about everything, cosmically speaking. Thinking about Buddhism—and/or trying to practice it in my lame fashion—was making me unhappy, she said, and I had to give it up. "But if it's making me unhappy, it's only because I'm doing it wrong," I cried.

"So what?" my sister answered me. "So you're doing it wrong. Big deal. Just quit doing it."

My sister has always been very pragmatic this way. I followed her advice, tossed my zafu (Buddhist meditation cushion) into a closet, and concentrated on finishing my coursework, getting laid, and thinking about myself all the time if I felt like it. I abandoned myself to my fantasies of being clever, of coming up with the right remark at the right time, and of being devastatingly sexually attractive to everyone who struck my fancy. Who needs reality? Who needs satori? I thought. Fantasy is terrific.

I've never felt as bad about my selfishness since, but I still tend to think of it as selfishness, and, as such, the clearest indicator of my fundamental unwomanliness. But perhaps, as every friend I've ever had has told me, I was being too hard on myself. Maybe other women are as self-centered as I am but have found ways to appear otherwise. Or maybe I (or my mother, who instructed me on this point) made a fundamental mistake in my youth in thinking that having overflowing wells of empathy was a feminine trait, when it's really a maternal one. Indeed, I've never heard anyone talk about women's great sensitivity to others without explaining where it comes from. Where it comes from is always motherhood.

There are those who argue that it is simply women's biological potential to have children that makes them sensitive and nurturing. The uterus, a warm, nurturing place inside, radiates a kind of energy that brings out certain feelings in women: all women, even girls. Others believe that even young girls (obviously not yet mothers themselves) will tend to be more sensitive and nurturing because they identify strongly with their mothers. But there are those who think it is the practice of mothering itself that creates nurturing proclivities in women. Sara Ruddick, the author of *Maternal Thinking,* insists that it is the continual demand placed upon mothers to respond to a child's needs for preservation, growth, and training that bring out an empathic concern for others in those women who actually mother.

This would let me off the hook for my childhood, adolescent, and even postadolescent selfishness. But I'm a mother now, so it is high time that I start manifesting a profound selflessness.

Motherhood has in fact been a revelation to me. When my daughter Sophia was born, I felt instantly and permanently bonded to her. She was a gift from the universe, a sacred trust. I felt it was my absolute duty to care for her and love her and protect her to the very best of my ability and beyond. You can't beat that for maternal. Who would have believed it of me, a not-all-there woman? There I was in the delivery room, looking at a seven-pound baby covered in vernix, ready to abandon all thought of myself in my effort to give her everything I felt she deserved from me, which was, in a word, everything.

It didn't last though. Being around that baby on a day in, day out basis during the three months when I was on maternity leave made me want to go stick my head in the toilet and flush. It was intolerably boring, for one thing. My husband, Jon, came home from work one day when Sophie was about two months old and told me that a coworker of his had said, "Oh, isn't it the most wonderful age? I remember being home with my babies then. I'd lie there and look at them, and stroke their little hands, and when I'd look up, two hours would have gone by!"

"Wow," I told Jon, "you know, it's just like that for me too! I finish feeding Sophie and I lay her down on a blanket and gaze into her perfect, alert eyes. And I swear, I'm completely taken up by this overwhelming feeling of love and devotion, like nothing I've ever known. And when I look up, two minutes—sometimes even three!—have gone by!"

There were other signs of my unwomanliness, my unmotherliness, way back when I was in labor. When Sophie was still a baby, Jon and I watched a movie on television one night. It was about a couple expecting their first baby. Toward the end of the movie, the placenta starts peeling loose prematurely and the mother-to-be begins to bleed profusely. She's rushed to the hospital, and as she is being wheeled into the operating room for an emergency C-section, she keeps pleading with the doctors, "please save my baby, oh please save my baby," right up until they shove a gas mask over her face to knock her out for the surgery.

I turned to Jon there on the couch next to me. "Do you think it's a reflection on my suitability for motherhood that when I was in a similar situation"—going in for a C-section—"I was saying to the doctors, 'please don't let me die, oh please don't let me die'?" It wasn't even an emergency in my case. It's just that I was filled with an unholy terror at the thought that someone was about to cut my abdomen open with a knife while I was wide awake. Now this seems a perfectly appropriate reaction to me, but it is not one that women (read: mothers) are supposed to have. We are supposed to think only of the precious tiny life we are carrying. But I'll tell you, if a Catholic moral theologian had been in the delivery room and asked me whether mother or baby should be saved if only one could pull through, I wouldn't have hesitated for a moment. "I don't care what you do," I would've said. "Put a noose around its little neck and haul it out of me—just don't let me die!"

Still, the emotions that motherhood has engendered in me are overpowering. The desire to dismember anyone who interferes with my daughters' happiness is incredibly visceral. I'm a lifelong pacifist. But more than once I've found myself growling into their tiny ears (when they're too young to repeat what I say, or are fast asleep), "Honey, anyone fucks with you, I'll tear them into a million tiny pieces. You just tell mama, and I'll make them sorry they were ever born."

It's such a pleasure to find myself feeling like a normal woman without even trying. It really helps to make up for that linear thinking and those hairy legs. But in all honesty, I haven't noticed that my husband feels significantly different about our daughters than I do. He's very passionate about them. Our zeal to protect them surfaces at different times and places, but overall we're very closely matched in both the degree and the frequency of our maternal passions toward our children. Okay, I come out ahead. But not by much. Certainly not by so much that I would suspect that some deep compulsion attached to our different sexes is acting itself out in our respective psyches. If this fierce protectiveness toward my children indicates that I'm a woman, well then, Jon is a woman too, penis and all.

There's still more to this feelings thing though. Women are supposed to have more feelings, and finer feelings, and a greater sympathy toward others than men have. But closely allied to this is women's avowed tendency to believe (or feel?) that relationships are the main thing in life, the very stuff of which their identity is made. Women are women because they are sisters, daughters, mothers, girlfriends, wives, aunts, grandmothers, neighbors, acquaintances. They are women because they live within a web of relationships to others. And unlike men, so the argument goes, women are acutely aware of their entanglement in the web and continually work to secure their place within it.

The underpinning for this belief, like the one about the inherent maleness of language, also goes back to Freud, though it branches off in an Anglo-American direction rather than a French one. This school of post-Freudian thought, called object relations theory, begins as the French one does with the idea that both boy and girl babies are initially unable to distinguish between themselves and their mothers. Again, when the boy gets old enough to notice that he and his mother have different types of genitals, he switches his gender identification over to his father (or maleness in general). To become who he must be he has to break away from his relationship with his mother. This, the theory goes, is why men grow up to be relationship-breakers, why they strive to keep other people at a safe emotional distance, and why they end up defining themselves in terms of their work or their sports team or their beer consumption.

Object relations theorists describe a different experience for girls. Girls don't have to do anything to achieve a feminine gender identity except to stick with mom and let nature take its course. All the girl has to do is to keep sustaining and creating relationships like the one she first experienced with her mother. This is why women grow up to be "relational." This propensity to be relational is also used to account for women's "different moral voice," which, according to researcher Carol Gilligan, is not based on the sort of legalistic working out of notions of justice that characterize men's moral reasoning, but is centered instead on negotiating conflicting responsibilities and maintaining an "ethic of care" for all the parties involved. Once again, men imagine themselves to be autonomous moral agents while women perceive themselves as inextricably bound up in the lives of others.

You may have noticed that this entire theory of women's "relationality" is contingent on children's primary "object"— the person through whom they first orient themselves in the world—being female: a mother. The child's experience, and thus their propensity to be autonomous or relational, derives from whether or not the child's sex is the same as that of their primary object. Some object relations theorists think that the mother is necessarily the infant's first object, that this relationship stems from the biological facts of pregnancy. The fetus is inside mom, and when it comes out and is a baby, it still wants to be close to her. It might tolerate other caregivers, even male caregivers, but it knows where home is, and that's as close to mom as it can get without crawling back inside. But Nancy Chodorow, who has done more than any other feminist to popularize this theory of female attachment and male detachment, argues that infants perceive the mother as their first object as a by-product of our social conventions regarding women as primary child-rearers. The whole gnarly knot and all its consequences, including men's propensity to be relationship-breakers or distancers, would be undone, just like that, if men would take up their 50 percent of the parenting burden right from infancy.

It's a lovely theory. It makes a certain intuitive sense and has the virtue of being very hopeful where the future (or not) of sexism is concerned. What's made it difficult for me to accept this theory is that my life hasn't felt like this to me. It hasn't been all about creating and sustaining relationships and nestling safely inside them. It's been about that, but also about escaping relationships and reveling in the freedom I purchased for myself by doing so. Certainly my relationships are incredibly important to my life. I shudder to think that some horrible calamity might set me outside of them. I'd have to start over from scratch. I would become someone new, and I imagine that who I became would have a lot to do with whom I chose to forge new relationships with.

So far, so good. I am sounding like one heck of a woman. But for a female who grew up in an intact nuclear family with a breadwinner father and stay-at-home mother, I developed a surprisingly powerful desire to be free and independent, even at a young age. As a teenager, I remember trying to identify with the good-girl stand-by-your-man songs, but actually I resonated much more strongly with love-'em-and-leave-'em songs. An early favorite was a Gordon Lightfoot song called "Ordinary Man." "Try and understand," it went, "I'm not your ordinary man." As I sang along, I did not think of myself as the singer's sweet, martyred girlfriend who is repeatedly left behind, trying to understand. No, I was the titular not-your-ordinary-man, my biological femaleness notwithstanding. Years later it was Dwight Yoakam: "I'll be gone in the morning, in the morning I'll be gone, 'cause I'm not one for hangin' on; please don't think, girl, you've done something wrong, in the morning when you wake and find me gone." Again, I was not imagining myself as the loving woman waking up to an empty bed after a single night of passion with a restless cowboy. Nope, I was Dwight, out the door, good-bye, it's nothing personal darlin'. I knew this was a little odd for a woman. I tried to put myself in the gender-appropriate role as the girlfriend who stayed back home, embroidering doilies for her hope chest and waiting for Mr. Wanderlust to make his way back to her doorstep. The thought made me want to spit. Like I could *sit* in a *house* and *wait* for someone. Please. Time for me to go get on that midnight train.

I took lots of psychological tests in my twenties. Not because I was exceptionally crazy, but because I had no clue what to do with my life, and I went to one career counselor after another (whenever I could do so for free) hoping for insight. They all gave me personality tests. I answered the questions straight from my heart, as instructed, hoping for insight, and a week or so later, my personality profile would come back. The summary couldn't have been clearer if they'd stamped "MAN" in neon orange letters across the sheet.

I'm exaggerating. On the 16 PF Test Profile, which I took in my early twenties, I had one of the greatest femme moments of my life. I was three standard deviations up from the norm on the "tough-minded/tender-minded" scale, which meant that I was "tender-minded, imaginative, introspective, artistic, fastidious, and excitable" as well as being "demanding, impatient, dependent, and impractical." What a string of adjectives! I could be the heroine of a Thomas Hardy novel! One of those difficult, childish, and charming women that bewitches the stolid hero who can't pronounce words with more than two syllables but knows how to harness a horse, by god.

The Taylor-Johnson Temperament Analysis, which I took

when I was twenty-one, was ambivalent as to my gender. It reported on nine personality traits. On every single trait I was
rated "improvement desirable" or "improvement urgent,"
which in itself was distressing. But the specifics were also upset-
ting: I was found to be nervous, depressive, quiet, inhibited,
indifferent, subjective, dominant, hostile, and impulsive. Taking
a very broad interpretation, I'd say that being depressive, quiet,
inhibited, and subjective could all arguably identify me as female. Nervous and impulsive are a bit harder to call. But what
about indifferent, dominant, and hostile? We're talking macho
here. Of course, the labels that stung most were "indifferent"
(elaborated as "unsympathetic, insensitive, unfeeling") and
"hostile" ("critical, argumentative, punitive"). My minister,
who gave me this test, pointed out that this was not who I *was,*
but how I perceived myself to be. He suggested that as a coun-
terbalance, my then-boyfriend should take the test, answering
the questions for me, stating how he perceived me. I had placed
myself as "indifferent," in the twentieth percentile; he placed me
as "sympathetic," in the ninetieth percentile. One thing I will
say for men: they want so badly to believe that women love them
and care for them and feel for them that they will easily imagine it happening even when it's not.

The last time I submitted myself to a personality profile was
when I was nearly thirty years old. All those menstrual cycles
and all that good clean heterosexual living had had no temper-
ing effect on my creeping psychological maleness. I was more of
a man than I'd ever been before. This time it was the Edwards
Personal Preference Schedule, composed of fifteen scales. The
psychologist, upon setting the results in front of me, said "Well,
I can certainly see why you haven't enjoyed being a secretary all
these years! You're definitely in the wrong line of work." But I
was way past remembering our ostensible purpose in doing this
test, which was to find a career for me that would suit my temperament. I was busy trying not to cry, because there it was, in
black and white, my worst fears about myself as a human being.

I was in the seventh percentile for affiliation, which included items like "to be loyal to friends, to do things for friends, to form strong attachments." I was in the nineteenth percentile for deference ("to find out what others think, to get suggestions from others"). I was only in the twenty-fourth percentile for nurturance ("to help friends when they are in trouble, to treat others with kindness and sympathy, to forgive others"). Meanwhile, I was practically off the top end of the charts in autonomy ("to be able to come and go as desired, to feel free to do what one wants, to avoid responsibilities and obligations") and achievement ("to be successful, to be a recognized authority, to be able to do things better than others"), and not far behind in exhibition ("to say witty and clever things, to say things just to see what effect it will have on others"—and worst of all, since my mother had tagged me with this particular sin literally since I was an infant—"to be the center of attention"). Oh, the horror ... the sheer, unmitigated horror.

At this point in my life, I was beginning to take some pride in my academic achievements, and I had nearly stopped castigating myself for failing to have five children who would be dressed entirely in clothes that I, their mother, had sewn for them by hand. But the Edwards Personal Preference Schedule hit me hard. The psychologist saw this. He tried to make me feel better by pointing out that the test designers used two entirely different sets of norms for ranking men and women. (I guess they didn't want women feeling bad when their desire for achievement came out somewhere in the tenth percentile solely because the curve had been wrecked by a bunch of type A, corporate-ladder-climbing men.) So my results were comparing me to other adult women only. The psychologist took out his tables and told me that I was not such an anomaly if you compared me to adult men. Then I was only in the eighty-eighth percentile for autonomy, in the twenty-fourth percentile for affiliation, and darned close to the fiftieth percentile for nurturance.

Oddly, I took some comfort in this. Yes, I was certainly no sort of woman, but if you put me in a great big hopper with all

the other people in the world, I was not the coldest, unfriend-
liest, most unfeeling person of all. As a guy, it turned out, I
wasn't bad at all. Not only did I show significant improvement
in certain strategic feminine categories like deference and nurturance, but my high scores in things like achievement and autonomy suddenly took on a fresh, happy glow. Maybe I was a
self-important, overbearing, hard-hearted woman, but if you
were willing to look at me from a different angle, why I was a
real go-getter of a guy.

There was another high-ranking category in my Edwards
profile that I probably ought to mention: heterosexuality. I was
in the eighty-seventh percentile for women on items such as
wanting "to go out with members of the opposite sex, to be in
love with someone of the opposite sex, to kiss those of the opposite sex, to participate in discussions about sex," and so on.
(As a man, I was still oversexed, but only in the seventy-third
percentile.)

I grew up in a funny time for women when it came to sex.
Premarital sex had become a required course, and the feminist
movement was busy teaching women to masturbate and insisting on the nonexistence of the vaginal orgasm. Pregnancy,
syphilis, gonorrhea, chlamydia, and herpes were all clear and
present dangers, but AIDS was not yet on the horizon. It was a
wonderful time to be young and single.

Sort of. Except if you were a woman, you couldn't sleep
with too many guys or you'd come to be regarded as the town
pump. An occasional purely recreational sexual encounter was
okay, but you had better be able to say afterward that you were
drunk. For the most part, you'd be playing it safer if you
confined your sexual exploits to men with whom you were having "a relationship." Women were supposed to want sex, enough
to engage in one-night stands now and again, but not so much
that they ever lost sight of the ultimate goal: love. Fortunately, it
was thought, with women's naturally lesser sexual appetites and
their innate yearning for connection, this was not too difficult.

My students tell me that this hasn't changed much in the last twenty years. There is still a supposition that men want sex all the time, anywhere they can get it, while women are more choosy, and able to be more choosy because, frankly, they're less interested.

This divergence between men and women is pure Gender 101. Everybody "knows" this to be true.* For example, in a recent study of whether smiling is perceived as an indication of sexual interest, researchers at Princeton found that men were more inclined than women to think that members of the other sex who smile at them want to sleep with them. The researchers put this down to projection and wish-fulfillment. They concluded—without a shred of positive evidence—that "everybody projects in this way, but since men are more interested in sex, they tend to overperceive sex in women."

I grew up with these same cultural stereotypes, of course, which is why I was so surprised to hear the results of a sex survey on the radio several years ago. I don't remember the exact figures, but trust me, these are in the ballpark. When asked how often they had sex, men said, on average, 2.1 times a week. Women said, on average, 1.7 times a week. (The disparity between the two being due to either a failure of accurate reporting or the statistically skewing effect of men having sex with each other more often than women do.) When asked how often they would *want* to have sex in the best of all possible worlds, men said on average 3.2 times a week and women said 2.9 times a week. The minute I heard this I thought, "These figures are so incredibly close!" But my reaction was short-circuited by the (female) radio announcer, who immediately remarked, "Well, isn't this just what you'd expect? What is it with men anyway? They're like a bunch of dogs in heat! Why don't they just get over it already? Am I right, ladies?"

Well no, I didn't think she was right. I thought that if you asked an average man how often he wanted to have sex, he

---

*Of course, it has only become true in Western society over the past couple of centuries. Before then it was well known that women were filled with insatiable lusts completely unmatched by men's comparatively tamer desires.

would think, "I'd better say a lot, or people won't think I'm a real man," and he'd add a bit to his figure. He'd be thinking, "Why just yesterday I was driving to work and thinking about Heather Locklear and it made me kind of hot, so I must have wanted it right then." Whereas an average woman would probably think, "Well, I like sex, but I'm not a nympho," and she'd subtract just a bit. She'd remember thinking that morning that the guy behind the counter at Dunkin' Donuts had a cute ass, but "It's not like I wanted to have sex with him!" she'd assure herself.

A recent *Us* magazine profile of "the world's sexiest athletes" shows the same pattern in how women and men assess their sexual appetites. Several athletes, male and female, were asked to rate their sex drive on a scale of one to ten. Olympic track star Marion Jones answered, "After I've lost a race, it'll be a one or zero. After a big win—sevenish." Gabrielle Reece, beach-volleyball player (and model) responds apologetically, "Six or seven. I'm so active, I think it can impede the sex drive. But I could go from having won a tournament to fooling around a lot sooner than if I got my butt kicked. When that happens, you're like, 'Honey, please.'" New York Giants cornerback Jason Sehorn also links his sex drive to his athletic endeavors, remarking that "on a day with no game, it's a straight up 10. Otherwise, it's 9.9." Race-car driver Helio Castroneves shows no such reticence: "Eleven," he says. "Why be modest?"

If you want to, I guess you could just tote this up as more evidence that men are more interested in sex than women are. But I find it hard to believe that this isn't more about fulfilling social expectations than making an honest assessment of one's level of sexual interest. Jason Seborn wants to sound like 215 pounds of virile masculinity; Marion Jones wants to make it clear that she's sexy all right, but she's no slut. To me, when men say they want sex 3.2 times a week while women vote for 2.9, it's functionally identical.

So do you trust the surveys or the stereotypes? The personality tests or the anecdotes or personal observations? How can we determine how femininely appropriate my feelings, my desires, or my mode of being in relationships are?

It's all a matter of perspective, of course. The reason I came up on those personality tests as a selfish, hostile, sexual person was because I answered questions over and over again saying "yes, that's me, that's what I'm like, selfish and hostile and oversexed." It wasn't that someone slyly assessed my inner state and concluded that my feelings were inappropriately masculine for a woman. Maybe the relevant question here is why a perfectly sweet and lovely girl like me could imagine herself to be such a fiercely independent, achievement-seeking, lover-leaving, pseudo-dick-wielding guy-in-a-woman's-body. That is, maybe it's all about my flawed self-assessment, not my actual personality.

But I don't think it's as simple as all that. I have the feelings women are supposed to have, practically all of them. A cutting remark can reduce me to tears; my heart goes out to my friends when they're in any sort of pain; the sight of roadkill makes me recoil in horror. But I have other feelings too, ones that are not deemed feminine. The desire to dismember anyone who hurts my daughters passes the feminine test with flying colors. It is the exception that proves the rule. But the desire to dismember the jerk who sits in the left-turn lane right through the yellow light is something else again. Why am I thinking "That idiot! Die, fool, die!" instead of "Poor man, he must be very nervous about driving." Hasn't my brain been basted in estrogens for enough years by now that I automatically give over with the appropriate feminine feeling?

Except, of course, that the appropriate feminine feeling might be a fiction and have little to do with how women really react to situations. Just as facial hair can't, by definition, be unfeminine if most women have it, it's hard to see how sexual desire or a craving for success or irritation at a lousy driver are signs of an untoward masculinity if these are common feelings among women. And I think they are. Maybe I just choose my friends carefully, but I don't know any women who, when trying to make a left turn, say of the slowpoke in front of them, "Poor man, he must be very nervous about driving." Not when they want to get somewhere in a hurry, which in this neck of the woods, is all the time.

Are other women worrying that their feelings aren't appropriately feminine? Or do they assume that if they're having these feelings, then they must be feminine, because after all, they're women? Or do they not notice that they're having these masculine feelings, and therefore they can easily maintain for themselves the illusion that they're feminine? Maybe when that good friend pats my hand and says, "Oh Cynthia, don't say that! You're a wonderful person!"—just like a woman is supposed to—she's thinking "What a loser this chick is!" but she goes right ahead and takes credit for being empathic and nurturing, while I, in the same situation, would know myself to be a heartless misanthrope because of my true, deep feelings.

Feelings are tricky. Who knows what's really going on inside another person? Luckily, there's another court of appeals, one more tangible than feelings, and that's behavior. Do I act like a woman? What does a woman act like?

CHAPTER 4

Walking the Walk:
Acting Like a Woman

If asking whether I feel the way a woman is supposed to feel leads to endless introspection, questions about my behavior are more straightforwardly external. They can be tested by others. Indeed they have been, at least from the time I hung out on the elementary school playground, and probably before. I couldn't have been much past the third grade the first time someone posed a few simple challenges to me during recess. "Look at your fingernails," an acquaintance demanded. "Look at the bottom of your foot," she went on. "Show me how you strike a match." I didn't begin to understand what she was trying to determine with this series of instructions. But the mystery didn't last long. As soon as I'd done the things she asked, she explained that she was finding out if I acted like a boy or a girl. A girl observes her fingernails by holding her hand out at arm's length, palm down, as if admiring a ring on her finger. A boy, on the other hand, will curl his fingers back toward himself, as if in a fist. Girls seeking information about the bottom of their feet attain it by kicking their foot up in back of themselves and looking over their shoulder at its demurely displayed sole. Boys, who will spread their legs whenever without the slightest shame, stick their leg out in front of them and turn their foot upward, as if going into half-lotus. When it comes to matches, boys embrace danger: they strike toward their bodies. Girls, naturally, strike away.

Being a rather cautious little girl, I passed the match test.

But, as a dyed-in-the-wool leg-spreader and fist-maker, the foot and fingernail tests identified me as a boy. These gender-crossing errors were obviously the point of the test, because it caused great hilarity among my classmates when I displayed these boyish behaviors. That hilarity was quadrupled for boys who made the fatal error of striking the match away from their bodies or who (much worse) inspected their feet over their shoulders and their fingernails with an outstretched arm. They were faggots.

I'm quite sure that at that age I didn't know what a faggot was. I thought from the context that it must be like being a sissy. No one wanted to be a sissy. But if you were a girl and you were a sissy, it just meant you were annoying. If you were a boy, it meant that you weren't really a boy, or that you were a boy who was messed up in some horrible and permanent way that appeared harmless enough, but somehow perpetually excited the disgust of others.

Maybe "permanent" is an exaggeration. But a reputation as a sissy could definitely dog a guy right up through high school, and for all I know, beyond. I moved to a different town after high school, so I didn't get to do the longitudinal study on how sissy boys fare in adulthood, but I'll bet it wasn't well. Oh, maybe they've grown up to have fulfilling relationships and loving families and run big companies and drive BMW convertibles. But that doesn't mean they're not still sissies, and more important, that they don't *know* that they're still sissies, however many people they've fooled since elementary school.

I'd like to think that in the years since I grew up in the late 1960s the gender police have loosened their grip on the playground. But they haven't. It's as bad as ever, as near as I can tell from the outside. When my friend Lori's son Eli was in his preschool years, he was watching cartoons on television one afternoon with his older brother Joseph and Joseph's friends. A commercial for Barbie dolls came on. Eli watched in rapt fascination. "Mommy, Mommy!" he called to the other room. "Mommy, come look! That's what I want, I want a Barbie doll." At this, Joseph and his friends went into a veritable seizure of derision: "Eli wants a Barbie, Eli wants a Barbie," they singsonged at him. Eli listened to these taunts for maybe fifteen seconds before he started to shout, "Yuck! Barbie! Gross!" Because he was a very bright little boy, he recovered fast: "I was just joking," he insisted. He laughed louder than anyone. Of course he didn't want a Barbie; Barbies were for *girls*. Needless to say, Eli was never caught clamoring for a Barbie again. He avoided Barbie dolls like the plague—which, in terms of his constantly-under-inspection developing masculinity, they were.

That was nearly ten years ago. For a while more recently, I hoped that things were improving. Like when my friend Faulkner told me that her four-year-old son, Elijah, liked to wear nail polish. Lavender, no less. "And no one teases him about it," Faulkner exclaimed. "The kids are really cool with it." We were both pleased that the world seemed to be moving in a more tolerant direction, that four-year-olds, at least, could be innocent and free. But she called me back not two weeks later. Elijah came home that day and asked her to please remove his nail polish. She asked him what had happened.

"Nothing," he said. "I don't like nail polish anymore."

She wasn't satisfied with that answer, and she kept on probing him as she swabbed away at his fingernails with a cotton ball and acetone. It finally came out that a couple of girls had been teasing him about his fingernail polish. They told him that fingernail polish was for girls. "That's mean," Faulkner remarked. "How did it make you feel?"

"I don't want to talk about it," Elijah said.

So much for the brave new world.

The intersection between gender and behavior is a strange place to be. There are definite requirements. In many instances, they're right there in your face, no detective work required: like the no-Barbie-dolls-and-no-lavender-polish-for-boys rules. There are—as we parents of young children like to say—"consequences" for not adhering to the requirements. They are not pleasant. Indeed, they can work with savage force to guarantee near-instant compliance. I'm told that the Japanese have a saying: "The nail that stands up shall be pounded down." We pride ourselves on a much higher degree of individual freedom and tolerance for eccentricities in America, but when it comes to gender, there are some very hard and efficient hammers at work to pound any wayward nails down. Think of Eli, whose love affair with Barbie was so abruptly and brutally ended, never again to emerge, not even in whispers. The last time I saw Eli's room it was covered in footballs and soccer balls, from pillows to wallpaper. I think Eli likes sports more than I do, but regardless, I think he made the right choice in interior decoration. In his shoes, I would've done exactly the same. Given the consequences attendant on defying gender requirements, it's no mystery that people come to fulfill them, to one degree or another.

But where did the requirements come from in the first place? I ask this not in the huge cosmic sense of when in the evolutionary timeline gender first arose, nor in the nitpicky particular sense of who decided that Barbie dolls and lavender nail polish were only for girls. No, I'm after the stupid, unanswerable question here: which came first, the chicken or the egg? Did we notice that certain behaviors seemed to come naturally to men and women, and so we came to label these behaviors "masculine" and "feminine" respectively? Or did we decide that certain behaviors were appropriate to men and women, respectively, and then train boys and girls into acting out these behaviors? On the one hand, you can say that because we're men and women we behave differently; or on the other hand, you can say that we're "men" and "women" because we behave differently—and here word order and scare quotes make a crucial difference.

I know this sounds like that tired old nature versus nurture debate all over again. It is. And the answer is, as always, both: gender is a result of both nature and nurture. It's both, and furthermore, the two can't be separated. Nature never happens in a vacuum. There's always an environment. The fetus has its placenta, the baby has its family, the adult has its bridge club. The aphid has its ecosystem, and inescapably, so do we. So what's the point in raising the nature versus nurture question yet again?

I ask it because there are issues of volition at stake here, questions of self-consciousness, and I find those quite interesting. Let's take one of my more feminine behaviors as an example: I laugh at other people's jokes even when they aren't funny. Do I do this because I'm a woman and women value relationships and are therefore willing to giggle mindlessly because it makes others feel more comfortable? If this is the case, then I'm clearly behaving like a woman. But what if I laugh spontaneously at the unfunny because I am a woman and I have noticed, subconsciously and over many years, that laughing at the unfunny is a part of women's behavioral repertoire? Fine: I'm still behaving like a woman. But what if I think to myself, "That's not funny, but I'd better laugh, because that's what women do in situations like this"? That is, what if I'm aware that I'm playing the part and am purposely thwarting my own inclinations so as to fulfill the requirements of the female gender role? I don't think there can be any doubt: I'm still behaving like a woman.

People without access to my inner states—that is, everyone, including myself—can't know if my polite laughter is a natural expression of my inborn femaleness, or the result of a lifetime of training in femininity, or simply the product of my conscious desire to appear feminine. We try all the time to distinguish between these possibilities, but it really is a great mystery which factors are at work, shrouded in layers of ignorance and behavior modification and subconscious denial. In some cases, it seems like we can tell the difference. Like if I'm a ten-year-old girl and I tell you that I'm looking at my fingernails at arm's length because I know you will laugh at me if I don't, that pretty much confirms a self-conscious, culturally acquired femininity, doesn't it? But maybe I tell you that I'm a girl who is faking it when I hold out my arm, just doing what I have learned is expected of me, when in reality, unbeknownst to myself, I'm not a "real" girl at all, but an AIS (androgen insensitive) girl with one X and one Y chromosome, and that's why I don't "naturally" evince the proper feminine behavior. Or maybe I tell you that it comes naturally, but I'm not remembering how many times my mother told me to do it exactly that way. Or maybe I sincerely believe that I do it unthinkingly—whether from inborn nature or early training, I don't know—but actually I'm conveniently repressing the nanoseconds of consciousness during which the electric currents flying through my synapses are shouting, "Don't curl your fingers up like that! Don't you remember what happened last time you did that? You can't risk that again! Act like a girl, for God's sake!"

Ultimate mystery notwithstanding, all I want to know now is this: Does my behavior get to count as womanly if I'm behaving that way with the conscious intention of making you believe that I'm womanly? I have to know the significance of this. Because if behavior matters, but conscious intention does not, then I'm unquestionably a woman. Enough of my behaviors line up on the feminine side to tip the balance in that direction. But if conscious intention matters, and I'm some sort of man-in-women's-behavioral-clothing, then my femaleness is not so far above reproach. We've already seen that as a child I couldn't look at my fingernails or the bottom of my feet in the proper feminine manner without aggressive coaching. Indeed, if you walked into my office right now and asked me to look at the bottom of my foot, I can virtually guarantee you that I'd bend my leg up in front of myself and turn my foot toward my face. It seems the more natural way to me. Unless I remembered the secret meaning of this test. Then I would bend my leg up in front of myself and turn my foot toward my face, and when you told me triumphantly that that's how *men* look at the bottom of their feet, I would tell you to go fuck yourself.

This suggests yet another layer to the behavior question: What does it mean when you know the rules about how women act, whether consciously or subconsciously, and you *still* don't act like a woman? Does it mean that the behavior is so deeply contrary to your predilections that you can't follow the rules even though you know you should? Or does it mean that you've crafted a set of behaviors that, when considered in toto, leave you convincingly in the female camp, so you can claim a little wiggle room here and there without worrying about the consequences? Or does it mean that you've decided that the goal —appearing to be a woman—is not a worthy one, and that you will not make your behavioral decisions with that criterion in mind? I'd love to tell you that that's what I do, but I'd be lying. I've escaped the elementary school playground, but as the bard once said—didn't he?—all the world's a playground. I wouldn't dream of setting myself up for the kind of grief I'd get if I ceased to factor gender appearances into my decisions about how to behave.

My friend José tells me that the reason I continue to conform to female behavioral gender expectations in spite of my strong conviction that they are arbitrary is because I want to sleep with men. It is sexuality, he says, that is the secret engine behind my day in, day out performance of femininity. Otherwise, he reasons, I wouldn't bother. I'd be my mixed-up androgynous self and let people make whatever they wanted out of my "gendered" behavior.

He has a point. The gender I see in José's behavior, in his physical appearance, the way he moves, the way he talks, is unquestionably male. He's masculine even by straight standards, and he's gay. But he has told me that if he had to shave his beard and grow out his hair and wear dresses and giggle a lot in order to sleep with men, he'd probably do it. To his way of thinking, it's a reasonable price to pay: sexuality trumps gender, at least in his case and in mine.

But I'm not sure that this is valid for most people. I have a friend, Nancy. She doesn't want to sleep with men. She's a lesbian. People mistake Nancy for a man on a daily basis. "Here's your change, sir," they say, looking right into her face and dropping the coins into her hand. Even after extended face-to-face conversations, some strangers persist in believing her to be a man. This really annoys Nancy. She's taken to wearing little girlish hoop earrings in the hope that this will tip people off to her femaleness.

Why does she care? I suppose José might say that she wants to appear as a woman because she wants to sleep with lesbians. But I suspect it's less monodimensional than this. She wants to be perceived as a woman because this is who she feels she *is*. In clinical terms, femaleness is her preferred "gender identity."

The concept of gender identity was first developed by John Money, the same psychologist who encouraged Bruce Reimer's parents to raise him as a girl (though a similar concept was discussed by Havelock Ellis, a pioneering British sex researcher working in the early years of the twentieth century). According to this theory, individuals develop a stable internal sense regarding which gender they belong to, usually by the age of three or four. Some say that gender identity is strictly environmental, based solely on social cues. (For example, John Money thought this, which is why he felt so certain that he could convert Bruce to Brenda.) A child is identified as either a boy or a girl, and through a process of continued interaction with their social environment, they come to identify themselves this way. Others think that gender identity is partly a result of a person's social context but is also to some extent reliant on physiological sex or brain chemistry.

Whatever the ultimate source of gender identity, everyone agrees that physiological sex and gender identity may not match. These are the terms that have been used for years to explain the phenomenon of transgenderism: men who have a female gender identity, women who have a male gender identity. It also used to be believed that homosexuality was rooted in such "errors" in gender identity. Thanks to the gay liberation movement, it's now accepted that you can be a man with a male gender identity and yet want to sleep with men, or be a woman with a female gender identity and yet want to sleep with women. That is, sexual orientation has been detached from the old triumvirate of physical sex, gender identity, and sexual orientation, and the stool now stands on two legs in most people's thinking. But having a male body and a female gender identity, or vice versa, is still generally considered to be a more intractable problem than a bit of nonnormative sexual desire. For the last several decades, the prescribed treatment has been either psychotherapy aimed at changing the gender identity or surgery and hormone treatments aimed at changing the physical sex. Anything to make the two agree.

The interesting thing about gender identity, if you want to accept those terms, is that it can be quite profound, quite deeply rooted. Kate Bornstein, author of *Gender Outlaw*, used to be a man who had a female gender identity and who liked to sleep with women. Postsurgery (and accompanying behavioral changes), she is a woman who has a female gender identity and who likes to sleep with women: in other words, a lesbian. Before her surgery, Bornstein was warned that she might lose all orgasmic function when her penis was surgically crafted into a vulva. And yet she chose to go ahead with the sex change. For her, anyway—and in contrast to José's claims about himself and me—it would seem that gender identity was more important than sexuality.

But what of Bornstein's apparently less-than-absolutely-critical sexuality? Bornstein has always had a clear sexual preference for women, she says. If she were told that she would have to impersonate a man in order to have sex with women, would she do it? Well, by her account, that's exactly what she did for years. She impersonated a man. Having a penis undoubtedly made for an exceptionally convincing performance, but Bornstein got tired of the masquerade. She wanted to be seen for the woman she felt herself to be.

My friend Nancy also wants to be seen for the woman she feels herself to be. I asked her if she would be willing to dress like a man and act like a man if this were the only way she could continue sleeping with women. "Oh sure," she said. Sexuality over gender identity, just like my friend José. Then why does she react with injured pride when people think she is a man? The answer is really pretty simple: if people take her to be a man, there is always the danger that they will discover that they are mistaken. And this can be very awkward. Indeed, Nancy does not correct people who assume she is male. Quite the opposite. Once they have called her "sir," she tries to maintain the fiction—for example, by asking her girlfriend to pay for a purchase so the clerk who thinks Nancy is a man won't see "Nancy" on her credit card and realize his error. It's just too embarrassing. It's easier to allow yourself to be mistaken for a man than to watch confusion and possibly disgust ripple across the face of a stranger attempting to encompass the competing gender signals you present to them.

So why do most people act out the gender behaviors believed to be appropriate to them? Probably most simply because it's easier than rocking the boat. Gender crossing buys you a world of trouble.

Why then do some individuals act out gender behaviors believed to be inappropriate to them? Because sometimes you have to rock the boat.

Of course, the consequences of gender crossing aren't always so dire. If I look at the bottom of my foot by kicking my leg up in front of me, no one is *really* thinking I'm some sort of freakish she-man. And sometimes—for example, with sexuality, for some people—the stakes are high. It's worth making some waves.

I act like a woman, at times self-consciously choosing the approved feminine behavior whether those are my inclinations or not. Most of the time I probably act like a woman "naturally," either because these behaviors honestly come naturally to me or because I've practiced them for years. But why do I choose to act like a woman when I *don't* feel it suits me? I guess because I figure I have a much better chance of passing as a woman than as a man. As a rule, people desperately want you to present one gender identity or the other to them. Seriously, women have been murdered for trying to pass as men, and vice versa. Think of Brandon Teena, gang-raped and murdered when it was discovered that he was "really" a woman. His isn't an isolated case. There's Christian Paige, Marsha P. Johnson, Richard Goldman, Harold Draper, Cameron Tanner, Chanelle Pickett, Deborah Forte ... transgendered martyrs to society's obsessive desire to keep gendered lines firmly demarcated. If a little taunting by peers can make Elijah give up his beautiful lavender nail polish, what can the fear of death by violence accomplish? A darned good impersonation of a woman (or man), that's what. I'm not living in terror of a violent death because of my subjective sense that I'm not-all-there as a woman. But I also don't choose to publicly exaggerate the poorness of my fit. Indeed, I downplay it, acting like a woman when I can, ensuring that I don't push the limits too hard.

Okay, we've established that I'm trying to act like a woman. Am I succeeding? To answer that, first we need to know how women act. The rules aren't the same in all times and places. Sometimes you have to be veiled from head to toe. Sometimes you have to be showing skin almost everywhere. Sometimes you have to speak your mind. Sometimes you have to say things only with your eyes, with your glances. It can be very confusing.

To determine the basic outlines of what counts as feminine behavior these days, I consulted a friend's archive of highly gendered Internet jokes. The reason these things are supposed to be funny is that they rest on what we all "know" to be true about women and men. I figured this would direct me toward the most undisputed territory on the gender map in contemporary American culture.

Before sharing the results of my research here, I feel compelled to apologize: the jokes are not funny. At least I didn't find them so. Perhaps it is because I am a feminist of the nasty, pissy variety (Q: "How many feminists does it take to change a light bulb?" A: "That's not funny!"). In any event, you should feel under no compulsion to laugh.

Now, to what I learned. First, we have territory already covered. Women have more feelings than men, and their feelings are contradictory and confusing. To wit:

> A man finds a genie in a bottle. He gets granted one wish, and says, "I'd like to go to Hawaii. I've always wanted to go, but I'm afraid of flying, and even on a boat, seeing all that water makes me claustrophobic. So I'd like to have a road built from here to Hawaii."
>
> The genie says, "I don't think I can do that. Do you have any idea how far the pilings would have to reach to get to the bottom of the ocean? How much asphalt would be required? Sorry, it's too much to ask. Is there anything else you'd like to wish for?"
>
> The guy thinks for a minute and says, "Yes, there is one other thing I've always wanted. I would like to be able to understand women. What makes them laugh and cry, why they are temperamental, why they are so difficult to get along with. Basically, what makes them tick."
>
> The genie considers for a few minutes, and replies, "So, do you want two lanes or four?"

The greater feelingness of women is also confirmed in a list of reasons "Why It's Great to Be a Guy," which include

- You never have to worry about others' feelings.
- One mood, all the time.
- You can watch a game in silence for hours without your buddy thinking, "He must be mad at me."

Internet jokes also confirm the supposition that men are more interested in sex than women, as in the title of this "training course" for women: "Sex—It's for Married Couples Too." The extent of this difference in sexual appetite is thought to be so extreme that in the preliminaries to another joke, it alone is used to account for the multitudinous differences in behavior between women and men:

> All babies start out with the same number of raw cells which, over nine months, develop into a complete female baby.

The problem occurs when cells are instructed by the chromosomes to make a male baby instead. Because there are only so many cells to go around, the cells necessary to develop a male's reproductive organs have to come from cells already assigned elsewhere in the female.

Recent tests have shown that these cells are removed from the communications center of the brain, migrate lower in the body and develop into male sexual organs.

According to the joke, these differences between male and female brains manifest in childhood behavior: "Little girls will tend to play things like house or learn to read. Little boys, however, will tend to do things like placing a bucket over their heads and running into walls." After puberty, it explains, "Women think with their heads. Male thoughts often originate lower in their bodies where their ex-brain cells reside."

Yeah, yeah, we get it . . . men are ridiculously horny. We also learn that they're none too bright, which, interestingly, is another common theme of the highly gendered Internet jokes. I think we have to count this as a legitimate, joke-confirmed behavioral difference between women and men since it arises so often. Women are capable and sensible, and men (who in these jokes are pretty much always married to women in a standard Ralph and Alice Cramden arrangement) bumble along in their wake. A quote from Charlotte Whitton has been made famous on buttons and bumper stickers: "Whatever women must do they must do twice as well as men to be thought half as good. Luckily, this is not difficult." Or as Margaret Thatcher says in a quote that circulates routinely on the Internet, "In politics, if you want anything said, ask a man—if you want anything done, ask a woman."

Apart from feelings, sexual appetite, and general competence, the most commonly reiterated behavioral differences between women and men in Internet jokes fall into five categories: clothes, hygiene, housework, telephone habits, and driving.

First, clothes: women have a lot of them and always feel they need more, as in this training course for women: "Classic Clothing: Wearing Outfits You Already Have." What is true of clothes is especially true of shoes. One of the "Top Ten Things Only Women Understand" is "Why it's good to have five pairs of black shoes," while one reason why it's great to be a guy is that "Three pairs of shoes are more than enough."

When it comes to hygiene, women got it, men don't. It's great to be a guy because

- You can be showered and ready in ten minutes.
- The occasional well-rendered belch is practically expected.
- The world is your urinal.
- You can "do" your nails in minutes with a pocket knife.

Speaking of fingernails, this is how men score (or lose) points with women:

- You trim your nails +5
- You trim your nails in the living room −10
- You trim your nails and flick them at the cat −15

Housework is also a no-brainer. Women's standards are incomparably higher than men's. It's great to be a guy because

- You can leave a hotel bed unmade.
- You never have to clean the toilet.
- You don't have to clean your apartment if the meter reader is coming.

And training courses for women include

- Household Dust: A Harmless Natural Occurrence Only Women Notice
- Overcoming Anal Retentive Behavior: Leaving the Towels on the Floor
- Integrating Your Laundry: Washing It All Together

Now can you guess who talks more on the phone? Among the top ten things only women understand is "Why a phone call between two women never lasts under ten minutes," while it is great to be a guy because "Phone conversations last thirty sec-

onds." Training courses for women also address the telephone issue ("Telephone Skills: How to Hang Up") as well as the more
general phenomenon of female chattiness ("Silence, the Final
Frontier: Where No Woman Has Gone Before").

Finally, women can't drive. Training courses to address this
problem include

- Driving a Car Safely: A Skill You Can Acquire
- Introduction to Parking
- Advanced Parking: Reversing into a Space

Interestingly, many of the reasons given for why it's great to
be a guy have to do with women being discriminated against,
being the targets of sexism. Such reasons include

- Your last name stays put.
- You have freedom of choice concerning growing a mus-
  tache.
- You get extra credit for the slightest act of thoughtfulness.
- Car mechanics tell you the truth.

But I digress. These all have to do with others' behavior toward you, the topic of the next chapter.

So how do I fare in these principal behavioral categories of
Internet joke-defined femininity? Well, I have lots of clothes
and more shoes than I need. I bathe every day, groom my nails
regularly without playing silly games with the trimmings, and
attempt not to belch in public. Towels belong on towel racks,
where they can dry rather than mold, and toilets must be cleaned
regularly, owing to the activities that routinely take place there.
On the other hand, I do not make beds, hotel or otherwise, nor
do I worry about dust until it has accumulated significantly; I
don't clean up for meter readers, and I wash my laundry in whatever order it arrives on the floor.

You can see that my performance as a woman started out
well with clothes and shoes and hygiene but is now sliding pre-
cipitously in the housework category. But once we start talking

about telephones, it's only going to get worse. While I am perfectly capable of an extended phone conversation with a good
friend, I have a generalized horror of the telephone. I send
e-mail whenever I can and pray that whoever I am writing to
will respond in kind and not, god forbid, call me up. When I
have to make phone calls, and an answering machine picks up, I
erupt in spontaneous prayers of thanksgiving as I wait for the
beep, knowing that I can say my two sentences and hang up
without talking to a human being. If I need to call my optometrist to schedule an appointment, I do not pick up the
phone. Oh no. I write "make appointment with optometrist"
on my to do list, and wait for a moment of exceptional extro-
version to arise. (This usually takes a week or two.) Whenever
my husband is home, I make him answer the phone, even if he
is in the shower and I am lying on the couch. When my husband
suggests that I might call up the parents of one of our daughter's
friends to set up a play date, I look panic-stricken and promise
him sexual favors if he will make the call himself.

That's phones. As for driving, I'm a born and bred Califor-
nian. Which is to say, I'm a fabulous driver. I could parallel park
a pickup truck into a compact car space while blindfolded.

Tote it all up, and behaviorally, I guess I'm a hermaphrodite.

Now do I really have to explain why this is ridiculous? Anyone who has had more than two or three roommates can tell you
that the ability to see dirt is not a gender-specific trait. I have
lived with women who think that scouring the bathroom need
not be done more than once every few months, and I have lived
with men who have all their foodstuffs lined up in the pantry
by category and height with clear labels applied in indelible
ink. Same goes for hygiene: I've lived with women who see the
weekend as a welcome respite from their daily ablutions, and
I've known men who shower twice a day, every day, 365 days a
year. I have a woman friend who wears the same clothes several
days running and can never be bothered to buy more until the
old ones fall apart, and an ex-boyfriend who could never resist

the lure of a nicely pleated pair of slacks, no matter how many were already hanging in his closet.

Do I hang out with a crowd of gender misfits? I don't think so. I think I'm just more attuned to disconfirming evidence when a stereotype is at stake. I'm a contrarian. When someone tells me that men are exceptionally good at mechanical things, I don't think about my father, who is very handy; I think about my friend Abigail, who can take apart and put together just about anything with gears in it.

Perhaps you think none of this is very relevant, all this stuff about clothes and hygiene and one's relationship to telecommunication devices. These are *jokes,* ha-ha, let's not take them too seriously! I won't try to argue the analytical validity of humor here except to say that there is a worldview contained in these jokes, and every time they get told, it gets passed on as so much truth.

But all right, forget about the way I trim my nails or do my laundry. What about that greater constellation of behavioral traits that assure us that we're dealing with a woman or a man? You know ... boys are aggressive, physical, independent; girls are passive, emotional, interactive. The girls sit on the swings and make up nonsense nursery rhymes and argue over whose turn it is until they can all come to an agreement; boys climb up the jungle gym and try to see who can jump from the highest bar without breaking their legs.

I have two children, both girls. Think of my home as a mini-gender laboratory. One of limited scientific value. (This is a sample of *two,* okay? Not to mention that I have to be careful what I say, because these girls will grow up and blame all their troubles on the way I pigeonholed their personalities in writing when they were only ages six and one.) I regard both of my daughters as girls. I don't know what this means, of course. This entire book is premised on not knowing what it means. But I'm certain that it means something, this indefinable sense I have that I'm dealing with girls, and not with boys. I have no doubt that it leaks out in my behavior toward them in a thousand little ways that I'm only dimly aware of.

To some extent, I'm willing to let that happen without fighting it. I decided a long time ago that being a feminist and raising girls (or boys) would entail constantly negotiating a balance between permitting or even enforcing gender stereotypes and actively questioning them. If you tell your four-year-old daughter that you simply won't allow a Barbie doll in your house because they are twelve-inch plastic effigies of an unrealistic standard of feminine beauty that is racist, sexist, and classist and thus a symbol of everything that is wrong with the patriarchy and indeed the entire world ... well, I wouldn't want to be living in your house or paying your kid's shrink bills. I don't think I get the balance right all the time, not by any means. Who does? But I think you have to be willing to socialize your children into the gender roles that are out there in the wide world, because this is where they're going to live. What does it profit them, or you, to try to turn them into gender-neutral androgynes whom no one else will recognize as acceptable human beings? On the other hand, you want your children to be able to sidestep the mindless dictates of gender fashion, to know that their worth is not tied up in how well they do or do not fit the current gender stereotype. And if you're me, anyway, you want them to keep the feminist movement forging ahead for another generation or two or a hundred, however long it takes. That means helping them establish a certain critical distance from what the world at large has to say about gender.

This is all by way of preface, so you'll know what sort of parent I am and can take that into account as you read the following.

As a baby, whether by temperament or training, Sophie was a very social, very communicative child. She would happily sit in your arms all day and didn't like to be left alone. She never learned to crawl, and didn't bother to walk until she already had an impressive vocabulary under her belt. We never had to babyproof the house, because Sophie didn't voluntarily leave our sight until she was four years old. She wanted to be where we were, wherever that was. Not just in the same physical space; she wanted contact, conversation, all the time.

As Sophie grew older, she developed a clear fashion sense of her own. It did not include pants. Or shorts. She wore dresses or skirts every day, for every occasion: because she was a *girl,* she explained, and girls wore dresses. We pointed out to her all the girls she knew who wore pants every day, but empirical evidence was as nothing to her. She was not a *boy,* she would not wear *pants.* If we persisted in arguing with her, she would resort to the comfort argument. She liked dresses because they were more "comfortable." I bought that, up until I explained to her that even though it was just a stupid social convention, she would have to start wearing shorts under her dresses so as not to flash her underpants at people all day. She did this without protest. She could wear a T-shirt, shorts, and a skirt and be perfectly happy and, she claimed, "comfortable." But god forbid you should try to get her to take the skirt off, leaving nothing but the T-shirt and shorts behind. Then the level of her discomfort was appalling. When she was five years old I told her one night as I put her to bed that she would need to wear jeans to school the next day because her class was going for a hike in the woods. She begged, she pled, she cried, she refused to calm down until I relented and told her she could wear a dress if she wore jeans underneath it.

Did I mention that she throws a ball like a girl?

In short, Sophie has been, apparently effortlessly, what little girls are supposed to be.

For the most part. Other characteristics have surfaced, ones not so stereotypically feminine. We never had to fight the Barbie battle, or even present much Barbie counterpropaganda (although I do recall a discussion of the real-world unlikelihood of Barbie's bust-to-waist ratio), because Sophie never got interested in dolls. Occasionally someone would give her one as a gift, and she would make a big fuss over it for a day or two, and I'd think we were about to turn the corner into the doll phase. But then just as quickly she would consign it to a box in the basement, and we wouldn't see it for months and months, not until a friend of hers would come over and excavate it. Sophie loves the concept of having a little sister, and is coming to be more and more interested in Lucy as Lucy becomes more of a person. But I've watched Sophie's friends get all goo-goo-gaa-gaa over Lucy in a way that Sophie never has (except as a result of peer group pressure). I've seen her friends respond to a request to give Lucy a bottle with undiluted delight. Sophie has never seemed to regard caring for her sister as much more than an irritation, time away from more interesting pursuits. On the other hand, she's never been crazy about toy airplanes or trucks or anything like that. I can't, in honesty, count Sophie as a super girly-girl or a tomboy either one. She's somewhere in the middle.

Then there's Lucy. She's still young enough that I hesitate to venture much about how she will or won't slip into the suit of femaleness. But from the time she was three months old, Lucy would cry to be put down more often than she would cry to be picked up. She was on the move as soon as she could manage it. She's fascinated with objects, constantly picking them up and banging them into one another. She likes people well enough. She smiles at them, gives them big hugs, and babbles at them. But you don't want to get in between her and an object (and here we're talking *things*) of her desire. When other babies (or her mother) take things away from her, she grabs on in a death-defying grip and screams at the top of her lungs. When another baby is in her way, she gives them a shove and crowds on through. If she decides that it's time to climb over that big box on the floor, she keeps trying and trying, finding different angles and techniques, until finally she does it. She seems to enjoy the company of her family. But if she's got something going on on the floor of the living room while you're in the kitchen washing dishes, don't expect her to come looking for you.

Given my interest in the nature of gender, you'd think I would have figured out very early on that Lucy was a boy. But I didn't. She was a girl; a sweet, spunky little girl who knew her mind and stood her ground. I covered her in kisses and told her what a wonderful little girl she was. I imagined her growing up to become the Michelle Yeoh of her generation. It wasn't until she was crawling around the bedroom floor one morning when she was about nine months old that it occurred to me that, compared to Sophie anyway, Lucy was a textbook boy: physical, aggressive, independent, oriented to objects rather than people.

This realization was quite a thrill for me, since it confirmed everything I've always believed about the plasticity of gender. I shudder to think what would have happened to my fine set of gender theories if Lucy really *were* a boy. Would I say, "Oh my, I was sooo wrong about everything! Girls are girls and boys are boys, and never the twain shall meet. They come prepackaged, already little women and little men before they can even feed themselves." Luckily, I have not had to face down this specter and can remain confident that sex (as in the configuration of one's sex chromosomes) is only one relatively minor factor that influences an individual's behavior.

I definitely believe this to be true, yet I would never want to tell you that there aren't identifiable behavioral differences between women and men. They're often quite striking. For example, I sing in a community choir, and at the beginning of every rehearsal, we stand up, turn to the left, give the person in front of us a backrub, then turn to the right and do the same. Men who sing often feel they have something to prove when it comes to their masculinity, so maybe the usual tendencies are exaggerated in this case, but every week you see the same thing: women massaging slowly, quietly, persistently, staying in contact at all times, from the neck right on down to the waist, sometimes pausing to ask, "Is this okay?" Men do this too, when massaging women. But put them behind another guy and it's whap whap whap, one karate chop after another, hands never pausing and always returning quickly to home base (i.e., the guy's own body), while laughing loudly and jovially throughout. It's kind of pathetic, really.

Do I hear you protesting that these are social customs? That this is learned behavior? That in the Arab world men can kiss their male friends in public, walk down the street arm in arm, and never impugn their heterosexuality or be thought less masculine for so doing? Well of course they're learned behaviors! Do you think I was born with a desire to bathe every day and own lots of clothes, especially shoes? Look, I can remember acquiring these habits. I recall the exact car ride when my mother explained to me that now that I was approaching puberty, one bath a week just wasn't going to cut it anymore. I know when I decided that I needed more than three pairs of shoes. Ditto with clothes. In these matters, it was not femaleness per se but the acquisition of disposable income and a desire for social conformity that made this GWB (guy with breasts) into a woman. For all that, I'm still well behind most of my peers when it comes to my ability to dress myself. I'll find myself trying to choose clothes in the morning, wondering if what I'm considering is in style or appropriate to the occasion. I try to remember what other women wear, what I've seen other women wearing in situations similar to the ones I expect to encounter that day. I can't dredge up the information. I try to focus my mind on a single event, hoping that will sharpen my recall. "Last Saturday at synagogue," I tell myself. "You sat with a dozen women for an hour during the children's service. The service was boring. You were looking around the room at the other moms the whole time. Now what were they wearing?"

How should I know? They were in clothes. Dresses? Pants? I remind myself to take a better look next time, but it is only through such efforts of conscious attention that this information filters in at all. After I crossed the divide into my forties, I decided it was high time to dress like a grown-up, to stop shopping in the juniors department for rhinestone-studded T-shirts and low-slung jeans. But I didn't know how to dress like a grown-up. I'd find myself in a group of women, talking about what-ever, when I'd suddenly think, "Oh yes, look at their clothes, see what they're wearing, this is a great opportunity for field research!"

Is it supposed to be this hard, this forced? Perhaps, as I suggested earlier, my not-all-thereness as a woman is more about how consciously aware I've been of the process of learning femaleness rather than the simple fact that I've had to learn it. Really, everybody, from the hardiest biological determinist down to the most committed believer in the baby-as-blank-slate theory, recognizes that there are learned behaviors involved in gender. There's no other way to account for the phenomenon of femaleness being different in different cultures, of a particular trait being feminine in one culture and masculine in another. It's a question of degree, of how much of femaleness is learned and how much comes hardwired. I don't feel a particular compulsion to argue that none of it is hardwired. Maybe a lot of it is, more than I, in my feminist ardor, might want to imagine. But if indeed the whole structure of femininity is biologically hardwired, it hasn't been done by a master electrician intent on preserving the integrity of two separate genders. For one thing, there are a lot of people whose wires are apparently crossed. We've talked about the most extreme cases of this already: intersexes and transsexuals. But there are more minor cases of "miswiring" all up and down the line: girls who are aggressive, boys who are sentimental, that kind of thing. You meet them every day. They are in your towns; they are in your family. Impressively, these behaviors even persist in adult human beings who have been thoroughly indoctrinated into the rules for their gender.

It all makes me think that when we contemplate the visible face of gender, there's not that much under the surface that is clearly coded male and female. In other words, gender is not like an iceberg, with nine-tenths bobbing about portentously underwater, the mountain upon which rests the tiny spit of ice that the boat captain can see. Gender is more like a cathedral, with spires and turrets and gargoyles towering in rococo splendor over nothing but a few dozen rough-hewn, mismatched blocks set a bare ten feet under ground level. If we want to get at the reality of gender, a little prodding around the foundation in the scientific manner we reserve for getting down to the biochemical brass tacks of things is not necessarily a bad idea. But we should be realistic about what we're likely to find out down there. Because whatever it is, you can be darned sure it's not going to explain everything that's sitting on top of it. All kinds of things can be built on a foundation like that: femaleness, maleness, androgyny ... cathedrals, houses, palaces, mausoleums, shopping malls ... you name it.

At home here in the cathedral, swinging from the spires, I'd have to conclude that I'm a woman. True, I don't feel like the behavior comes as naturally as it seems like it should, but does that really matter? I walk the walk pretty well. I reflect on the women I know best: They have widely varying assessments of their own femininity or lack thereof, but they all strike me as idiosyncratic mixtures of female-appropriate behaviors and other traits, some of which are more appropriate to men. I would be hard pressed to say who among them is the more feminine. To me, their femininity seems to have most to do with how willing they are to believe their own propaganda. From this I conclude that I could probably behave exactly as I do now, and instead of feeling like I'm faking it, I could feel supremely confident in my femaleness. Probably no one would try to disabuse me of that notion. Put another way, the purposeful effort it takes for me to behave like a woman quite likely has more to do with my being neurotic than with my being unwomanly.

But it still disturbs me to contemplate how very manufactured my behavioral femaleness is. When other people regard me as a woman, I get the clear sense that they're imagining it to be a natural efflorescence of my biological femaleness. They're thinking I *am* a woman; I'm thinking I *act* like a woman.

This sense that I'm merely acting like a woman fits perfectly with one of the more popular theories about gender these days: performance theory. As the name suggests, performance theory argues that gender is best understood as an act. The issue of self-consciousness, on which I have dwelt at such length, is thought to be relatively insignificant in this formulation. We're all in

drag, the theory goes, whether we know it or not. We're all pre-
tending to be women (or men, if that's our role), observing and
mimicking what we believe to be femaleness. This extends from
our most personal, seemingly private encounters to our broad-
est social interactions.

Performance theory neatly transforms my neurotic dwelling
on the manufacturedness of my gender into an incisive hyper-
awareness of the real truth of the matter. You can see why I find
it appealing. According to performance theory, femaleness is
achieved, not given. It is only the continually repeated performance of femaleness that successfully establishes the fiction of its
ultimate existence. In other words, in buying lots of clothes or
laughing at the unfunny, I am doing my bit, however small, to
keep the fiction of femaleness intact. As I live in a time of changing notions about gender, one could even say that I'm doing my
part to nudge femaleness in this or that direction when I engage
in sly acts of subversion like avoiding the telephone or letting my
laundry pile up in the basement. Performance theory can be
very hopeful this way. Because theoretically, if gender is nothing
more than its repeated performance, we may be able to act out
other parts, to behave in such a way that femaleness comes to
mean something else or is rejected entirely in preference to some
other way of thinking about who people are. We start acting
differently, and lo, the world becomes a different place.

That's in theory. In practice, it's not nearly that easy. I can
act any old way I want, but it won't necessarily make anyone re-
think the category of femaleness. Ideas about how women are
supposed to behave are incredibly sturdy. Everyone knows that
women are expected to act differently in different cultures;
everyone knows that some large part of gendered behavior is
learned and in no sense inborn (for example, some people think
girls are born vain, but no one thinks they're born knowing how
to apply eye shadow). Yet almost everyone seems to labor under
the belief that women and men behave differently because they
are different. If we can all observe femaleness being learned and
then performed, if we can all see how arbitrary it can be, how

do we nevertheless manage to hang on to this belief that each sex has its own behavioral proclivities that you can't get around with any amount of feminism or gender-bending or other ill-advised, nature-defying ideological nonsense?

Actually, it's shockingly easy for human beings to maintain their favored beliefs when there are larger things at stake than "pure" knowledge ... which is pretty much all the time. There is a quote I love that describes this human capacity to push evidence into one's preferred theories no matter how poor the fit. It's from science writer Karl Sabbagh:

> I believe that the human brain has a ratchet, and it is one that swings into place whenever people are confronted with something they really want to believe in. Whenever they come across an example of a phenomenon that reinforces the belief they are interested in preserving, the mainspring of their belief tightens a little bit. But, if a little later they come across something that doesn't reinforce the belief, something that even contradicts the hypothesis they are fondly nurturing, the wheel rotates in the opposite direction but the spring doesn't loosen—it's still as tight as it was, and their faith is unshaken.

This is how belief in behavioral commonalities among women seems to me. The evidence for the existence of these commonalities is spotty and inconsistent. The world is saturated with women who don't fit the mold in one way or another. We have a hard time seeing this though. When a woman does an idiotic thing in traffic, we think "woman driver, it figures." All the women who are not doing anything idiotic in traffic don't count as evidence against the theory; they don't register at all. And when a man does the same thing in traffic, he's just a random idiot, not a typical "man driver." The theory stands even as the data around it bubble over with contradiction and counterexample.

I had my best education in these perils of interpreting data in 1981, the first time I saw a complete astrological chart for myself. Before that, I turned my nose up at astrology, as I had been trained to do in my scientifically minded family. I had a personal reason to doubt it as well: everything I had ever read about what Scorpios were like didn't sound much like me. Friends who were infatuated with astrology told me that I must be on the cusp or something, but I wasn't. My birthday was smack dab in the middle. Finally, at one of these friends' insistence, I got a book that treated astrology in a more complicated way. I drew up my chart, complete with aspects and houses and ascendants. Then I read all the little squibs from the book that were supposed to apply to me, and they did! It all sounded just like me!

I still couldn't explain *why* all this should be true, how the position of stars and planets at the time of my birth could actually make me and every other person born at that latitude and longitude at that time into little cookie-cutter people. I was troubled by my inability to come up with a suitable mechanism of action. But the evidence seemed incontrovertible. That chart had me pegged dead to rights. I drew up charts for several friends and read them their little squibs. They were amazed—it was all so true! I reported this enthusiastically to my parents, who told me, as I had assumed they would, that astrology was completely bogus. We argued and argued, and then I struck a bargain with my mother. I would draw up her chart and read her all her squibs. For each one, she would vote whether that characteristic was true of her, not true of her, or sort of in the middle. I would also read her the squibs from two other charts drawn up for people whom she did not remotely resemble. I'd read these to her in random order, and not editorialize, and we'd see if she picked her own chart as being most like her.

After I drew up her chart, I felt sure my mother would choose her own. It was her all over the place! But when we finished the exercise, my mother picked her own chart third out of the three I read as being most like her. That was not the most impressive thing, however; what was really striking was the distribution between what she thought was true of her, and not true, and sort of in the middle. It was virtually identical for the three charts. She thought more things I read to her were true of her than not, about 60 to 65 percent; that some 20 percent were both true and not true of her; and that the remaining 20 percent or so were definitely not true of her.

Made thoroughly suspicious by this, I went back and rated all the squibs from my own chart as to how well they did or didn't apply to me. It was a very graphic demonstration of how much counterevidence I had looked right past when I first read those squibs and felt that the stars had captured my personality so perfectly. There was a solid 30 percent that I couldn't say was true of me at all. Apparently when I read through my chart the first time, my brain had worked like a ratchet, tightening with every confirming squib and swinging free with every disconfirming one.

To me, the significance of this to the question of femininity is that if I go on a personal campaign to change the category of femaleness by performing it differently, there's an extremely good chance that I will be ignored. If I keep the bulk of my behavior and appearance within the limits for femaleness as it is currently constituted, my unmade bed and my slick parallel parking will be among those things that people see and yet don't see, that they observe but neglect to enter in as a data point when they are reflecting on how women behave.

That's if I make a sufficiently convincing case that I am a woman in the first place. If I flout too many rules too fast, I will be written off as a total aberration. I will quite likely be thrust into one of the categories that already exist for people who are apparently physiologically female but who don't act like women: you know, those who just can't marshal a convincing performance, or maybe don't see why they should try. People call them dykes. Or bag ladies. Or nutjobs. Once you're in one of these categories, what you do won't change anyone's idea of what female behavior consists of, since you're no longer counted as a normal woman.

I haven't engaged in this wholesale flouting of rules. I've

mostly acted like a woman, the more so the older I get. Perhaps I've acted like a woman for so long that I've internalized a lot of it. I'm more fluent in femininity and don't have to pause so often to think how to do it right. I guess you'd have to say that in my case, femaleness "took," at least enough to slip me past the bouncers at the door of Studio Woman.

CHAPTER 5

Who's Looking?
The Judgment of Others

The verdict of previous chapters is unanimous then. I'm a woman. I can wallow in angst from now until forever, I can thrust before you all the evidence of my not-all-thereness as a woman, but that's what I am, a woman. Maybe not the best, most textbook case, but no one is mistaking me for a man.

Well, not often. There was this one time a few years back when I was in a subway station in New York in the middle of the winter. I was wearing an enormous puffy down parka and my hair was no more than an inch or two long all over my head. The city was doing repairs on the pedestrian tunnels in midtown Manhattan at the time. I had no idea how to get where I was going below ground, but it was ten degrees outside, with a stiff wind blowing besides, so I was trying to avoid street level. Fortunately, there was a subway official standing in the station surrounded by people asking questions, so I went to stand in the circle around him to wait for my turn. As the other people got their answers and walked away, the subway official turned to face me. "Yes, sir," he enunciated clearly. "How can I help you?"

I ignored the "sir" and asked him how to get to Penn Station.

It was then that he decided I was a woman. I don't know what it was that tipped him off. The timbre of my voice? The purple mitten sticking out of my pocket? Perhaps it was the aura of femininity that I radiate from every pore unbeknownst to my self-conscious sour feminist persona. At any rate, the subway official realized that I was female, and he proceeded to fall all over himself apologizing—"I'm sorry ma'am, you were standing sort of behind me, of course you don't ..." and so on.

I kept saying, "Don't worry, it's okay, how do I get to Penn Station?"

He finally answered me, and I walked away, chuckling to myself over his reaction. As though his calling me "sir" was going to send me off to my bed crying for a week! What, I wondered, was so horrible about being a man that I should blanch at the prospect of being mistaken for one? It's not like he was mistaking me for a serial killer. I found this a most intriguing phenomenon, how frantic this man was to get me in the right gender category, and his deep solicitude for my feelings when he got it wrong. What a world we live in! I thought.

It turned out I had to go above ground to get to Penn Station. As I tried unsuccessfully to get my ears under the collar of my parka, I wondered if I really did look like a man. I didn't start to cry or freak out or anything. But I did keep turning from one side to the other, hoping to get a glimpse of myself in a storefront or the window of a parked car. I finally succeeded. I looked like a man. "Well, Cynthia, you've gone and done it this time," I anxiously berated myself. "With a face like yours you can't afford to cut your hair that short! What're you going to do until it grows out again?"

No one it seems, then, least of all me, is happy until they can get all the people they encounter popped into one hamper or the other, male or female. I think most of us are willing to tolerate a little gray area in the real-life permutations of physiological sex: people who have a missing testicle or an enlarged clitoris or an extra X chromosome. Quirky things happen; what are you going to do? But we want people to keep these matters to themselves and present a clear identity to the world, female or male, one or the other. What is so threatening about a bit of uncertainty regarding an individual's sex, about a gender that doesn't sit within one standard deviation of the norm for a particular sex? What is it that we have invested in maintaining a

strict gender system? Why has gender, or biological sex difference, if you prefer, taken upon itself such an enormous burden
of social and cultural stability?

I think that what is at stake is a system of social inequality.
We've all been taught that social inequality is a bad, bad thing.
There are some nice things about systems of social inequality
though. For example, you can decide quickly what you can expect from a person, how you should deal with them, whether or
not you have to take them seriously and under what circumstances. This truly is an advantage when you're meeting and in-
teracting with a lot of different people, as those of us who live
almost anywhere in the world today have to do. (Indeed, some
anthropologists speculate that systems of social inequality, in
which entire classes of people are taken to be subordinate to
other classes of people, are a relatively recent development in human evolution and a direct result of increased population den-
sity.) But I don't think I have to tell you what the downside
of a system of social inequality is, especially if you've spent any
time on the downside of a system of social inequality.

The system of gender inequality relies on being able to as-
sign a person an identity based on more or less easily observable
physical characteristics. The identity itself consists of much more
than those physical characteristics, of course. This is why I can
sit around brooding over whether I'm "really" a woman or not.
But the physical characteristics are paramount. If a man puts on
women's clothes and thinks, acts, and talks like a woman without actually trying to conceal his biological sex, no one will
decide that all things considered he's more like a woman than
a man, so that's the category he should occupy. He'll still be a
man. A transvestite. If I put on men's clothes, if I think like a
man and act like a man and talk like a man, but people can still
see that I have female sex characteristics, I will not be accepted
as a man. I'll be a cross-dressing woman.

A now well-known jazz musician, Billy Tipton, spent his
entire adult life as a man. He was so good at acting like a man,
dressing like a man, and so forth, that he fooled a couple of his

wives, not to mention everybody else. When he died, and his observable physical characteristics were brought into plain view, people did not say, "Wow, that was one really weird guy!" They said "Wow, that Billy Tipton was a woman all along! She was just passing as a man!" In other words, Billy's clothes, mannerisms, wives, manner of thinking, participation in a male-dominated profession—all things we think are part of being a man—were not enough to make him a man once his female body parts came to light. These characteristics instantly became secondary.

Am I now saying what I refused to acknowledge earlier, that biology is destiny, that sex is what you find between your legs? Yes and no. In a sexist society, biological sex is *used* to frame destiny. But biology alone, uninterpreted by culture, has no such highly determinative power. W. E. B. Du Bois, civil rights leader and founder of the NAACP, explained that where race is concerned, "the physical bond is least and the badge of color relatively unimportant save as a badge; the real essence of this kinship is its social heritage of slavery; the discrimination and the insult." As for race, so it is for sex. It's not what sex is; it's what it does.

I think that's the real reason why femaleness feels like an itchy suit of clothes to me. I have no trouble acknowledging that I have an XX chromosome configuration and the sort of primary and secondary sexual characteristics that are classified as female. But "woman" carries a lot more baggage than that. And I'm not allowed to accept the female classification without the baggage. Looking over my Edwards Personal Preference Schedule and deciding that I'm a pretty darn good man might be comforting to me, but those aren't the standards against which others are measuring me. They're looking me over, deciding I'm female, and then picking up the female yardsticks to decide how well I'm doing. I can pin a sign to my chest that reads "Guy With Breasts," but will people really look past the breasts and start treating me like a man? Of course not. It's the inescapability of gendered identity that makes it what it is.

Maleness is an inescapable identity too, one that harms a lot of poor unsuspecting human beings who happen to have penises. I don't think the damage done is strictly equivalent to that done to women. I don't buy the idea that we're all equally harmed by a two-sex system that refuses to deal with us as full masculine-and-feminine-but-let's-not-use-those-terms human beings. Women are systematically discriminated against. We are the underclass of the gender system. In fact, in a fit of hyperbole I would go so far as to say that that's what being a woman is: occupying that slot in society that has been reserved for women, a slot that is subordinate to men's.

Feminists have been wary of talking like this for the last decade or so. It seems to make femaleness equivalent to victimization. It *does* make femaleness equivalent to victimization. What's the problem with that? Well, we want to be able to say positive things about women. We want to talk about what makes us good, valuable people—like our nurturing, relational ways or our "natural" concern for ecology. We want to make sure that everyone knows that even under conditions of oppression, of victimization, women have been active agents: making choices, living lives, offering up resistance to the system of sexism in one way or another. Some people also want to make sure that we see how women have been complicit in sexism, how women have perpetuated the system and profited from it, so that we can correct those mistakes in the future.

All this is perfectly reasonable. I have no objection to highlighting these aspects of female existence. But I want to insist that what makes this existence "female" is only that the people labeled "women" have engaged in it. There is nothing about women's behavior under conditions of oppression that is uniquely "feminine," that is "womanly." Sure, we're more than victims! But only, and in exactly the same way that we're more than our constrained existence as "women" might suggest.

To sum up: to be a woman is to be consigned to a subordinate class on the basis of a few simple phenotypic markers. By comparison, everything else—the high heels, the weepiness, the

XX chromosomes, the telephone behavior—is just window dressing.

It's not that these things don't matter at all. But to behave as though my femaleness is primarily about my inner sense of how well I fit various stereotypes of femininity is to miss entirely the much larger reality of femaleness: that it is something that others decide about you. Am I a woman? Well, do other people think I'm a woman? Not do they think I'm a good woman or a bad woman, a feminine woman or a masculine one ... just, do they think I'm a woman? If the consensus view is that you're a woman, then for most intents and purposes, you are.

Who is a woman? All the people that we commonly agree to be women. How can you tell they're women? Because we commonly agree that they are.

You couldn't ask for a more circular definition of femaleness. Yet I think it's an accurate one. It captures to me what is the single most salient fact about femaleness: that it is an ascribed identity. It is not, first and foremost, an identity that you choose. It is an identity that is assigned to you, usually at birth if not before, and that trails you throughout the rest of your life (unless you opt for sex "reassignment"; then the other identity is ascribed to you, usually just as inflexibly).

When I say that femaleness is an ascribed identity, I don't mean to suggest that there's no choice involved in gender. There's actually a surprising amount of latitude, in my experience anyway. You can negotiate a lot of the details, express your femaleness in a variety of ways, choose to some degree where and when and even whether you want to accommodate yourself to gender-based expectations. And of course the expectations are different in different times and places. But you can't "unchoose" your femaleness. Not easily, and not without a perpetual fear of discovery or humiliation. To me, this is the core of what it means to be a woman.

Years ago a friend asked me which I thought of as my more defining characteristic: being a woman or being Brethren? Being Brethren—that is, belonging to the Church of the Brethren

—has been a profound source of identity for me. As a result of generations of intermarriage, my family tree does not branch out and out into ever vaster reaches of ancestral space. It turns back in and grafts itself on to its own limbs. My parents are fourth or fifth cousins. So were my paternal grandparents. For a long adolescent time, my sights were firmly set on finding a lanky, pale, near-sighted, neurotic, intelligent, fifth-cousin son of a Brethren minister (or, just as good, a Brethren farmer) to marry me and raise five or six pale, near-sighted, neurotic, four-part-hymn-singing children.

Things changed. By the time my friend asked whether I thought of myself as more Brethren or female, I was thirty years old and living a hundred and fifty miles north of the nearest Brethren church. I felt no special affinity for Jesus and was involved with a Jewish man whom I would later marry (and with whom I'm now rearing two Jewish children). I knew the answer my friend was fishing for: she was on the cutting edge of the feminist movement in the late 1980s, which meant giving up the misguided white feminist notion that all women were first and foremost *women,* whatever other identities—racial, class, religious—were layered on top like so much runny frosting. So I was perfectly free to name myself as primarily Brethren. It would have been the best thing to say, actually, an assertion of my ethnic specialness. ("No, no, I'm not your average white girl! I'm a special kind of white girl, and not the bad kind either!") And truthfully, I'm Brethren in my bones, in a way that far surpasses anything so superficial as attending church or reading the Bible. Certainly I have more in common with a Brethren man than with, say, an Ojibwe medicine woman.

But I couldn't claim Brethren as my primary identity because it wasn't. As I explained to my friend, even though I feel that I will always be Brethren at some level, there are lots of other levels. I can publicly disavow Brethrenism and everything it holds valuable. And if I do so, there are dozens, hundreds, even thousands of identities that can take its place (including catch-all categories like "nonreligious" and "unaffiliated"). Few people would seek to deny me these new identities, or to dispute my claim that I am no longer Brethren.

But being a woman is different. I can be a woman in a lot of different ways, but can I stop being a woman altogether? If I decide to regard femaleness as a former (if formative) identity, where else can I go? With a lot of effort, and possibly surgery, some liberal-minded people might regard me as a man. That's it. Two options, at the outside. And what if neither of those options is especially attractive to you?

Some brave souls try to venture outside the male and female boxes and stake out turf for a third gender, another gender, a blend of genders. Sometimes they are tolerated as benign freaks. In certain unique social circles, they may be hailed as hero/ines. But out here among the rank and file, such persons are usually taken to be "really" male or female, and the fact that they won't straighten up and act right—that is, appropriate to their assigned gender—tends to incite anger in others. Gender-bending may be a brilliant countercultural, antipatriarchal move, but it's also a good way to get yourself beaten up. No wonder most of us avoid it, even if it entails some real violence to the selves we wish to be.

That's femaleness for you: love it, hate it, embrace it, fight it, try to reason with it ... it'll still be there when you wake up in the morning. You're marked. For life. As the saying goes, "if you forget you're a Jew, a goy will remind you." That is, if you decide you're not a woman after everyone else has agreed that you are ... well, face it, you're still a woman in most of the ways that count. Because just as anti-Semitism is implied in the phrase, "if you forget you're a Jew, a goy will remind you," sexism is implied in the attribution of femaleness. To an impressive extent, the label "female" exists to make possible the social subordination of women, just as "race"—that is, the habit of categorizing different people according to skin color—exists mainly to make racism possible.

When I suggest that gender exists primarily as an assigned identity that has comparatively little to do with one's precise physiology, feelings, or behavior, I end up sounding like what is known in the gender theory trade as a "social constructionist." The motto of social constructionism is that women are made, not born. We invent gender, we act it out, and we reinforce it. We don't "discover" it, because it's not already there. Whatever existence it has is what we've given it. As mentioned earlier, the most radical gender theory these days goes further to argue that sex, biological sex, is every bit as socially constructed as gender is. Dividing physiological and reproductive phenomena into two categories and calling them "male" and "female" is an invention, a theory: a social construction. It may be a good theory, an explanatory one, one that conforms well to observable phenomena, but it is still a product of our minds rather than an unquestionable fact of nature.

When I'm in the proper philosophical frame of mind, this all seems quite evidently true to me. I believe it. But I can see why people have trouble with it. It's kind of like saying the earth is a round ball rotating on its axis and revolving around the sun. Forget for a moment whether or not this is the case; does it really *feel* this way to you? Is this how you experience the earth as you stand, sit, lie, swim, walk, or run over its surface? If you do, my hat is off to you; you possess a better imagination than my own.

I'm not trying to say that the earth is flat. Like everyone else reared in the West during the last several hundred years, I am convinced that the earth is round. Everything seems to point to that conclusion. If you buy into the assumption that the earth is a sphere held to its trajectory through space by gravitational forces, then the apparent behavior of planets and stars, tides and weather systems, airplanes and boats, all fall into a neat scheme that is both simple and comprehensive in its explanatory force. Or at least that's what I'm told. Minds far better than my own think the roundness of the earth is indisputable, and I am not inclined to argue with them.

But do I experience the earth as round? No. It's flat. Don't you think? When I stand and watch the sunset, is the ground on which I'm standing spinning rapidly away from a great fiery ball in the sky, gradually consigning to darkness the semisphere I call home? No. The sun is setting: that is, it is falling slowly downward through the sky until it slips under the horizon to the west. When I fly from New York to California, am I traversing a three-thousand-mile arc of earth? Doesn't seem like it. No matter how good the movie is or how badly I need a nap, I never go up in an airplane without looking out the window eventually, and the evidence of my eyes is clear: we are flying at a steady altitude over a flat surface interrupted only by mountains and canyons. The world is like a big sheet cake. The icing forms attractive peaks and valleys, but it doesn't wrap all the way back around to meet its own edges on the underside. I could get to China by tunneling through the earth? This sounded far-fetched to me in elementary school, and it still does. It would mean that the people in China would have to be hanging from the earth by their toes, since we here in America are standing upright.

Gender is the same way. I can get myself into a frame of mind where gender is entirely socially constructed, and wow, who would have believed it, so is sex! It's all interpretation, and no reality! It's all cathedral, and no foundation! Moreover, I can believe that this amazing towering structure that looks and feels so solid would crumble into dust—or really, into complete nothingness—the instant that we stopped clapping our hands for Tinkerbell and shouting, "I believe, I believe, I do believe in gender!" (or sex).

But I can't stay in that frame of mind for long. It's not my walking-around manner of thinking. Because I have a vulva and breasts, all the time, rain or shine. And I've met a lot of people who are called "men," and every one of them either has, or says he has, or doesn't deny having, this extra appendage called a penis. I look around, and I can see that people called "men" are more likely to be able to fix a broken washing machine, that they tend to walk with a swagger, that they're less willing to accept help from others. I can see that people called "women" are more interested in talking about Uncle Carl's gallstone surgery than men are, that they spend more time primping in front of mirrors, that they start a lot of their sentences with clauses like "I don't know, but . . . ." I can see that men make more money, own more property, and run more governments. I can see that women raise more children, mop more floors, and spend more time shopping. In short, the generalizations appear true; the stereotypes fit. Maybe they help to create the reality of gender, but they also reflect it, and pretty accurately too. Of course, they often fail to hold in individual cases. I've pointed out numerous places where I personally don't fit the stereotypes, and I've questioned how accurate they are overall. But as great statistical truths, some of these generalizations have real merit. Gender is a phenomenon whose existence cannot seriously be doubted.

How can we account, simultaneously, for this observed phenomenon of gender and the equally accurate observation that there are so many exceptions to the rules, so many women and men who don't conform to the stereotypes? The social constructionist answer is self-evident: we all learn to fulfill our gender roles, but some of us internalize them more completely; some of us are less willing to court social censure than others; gendered performances come more easily to some of us than others. But one needn't be a social constructionist to explain away the phenomenon of gender nonconformity. Say that men and women, the two sexes, are truly different from one another in profound ways, for any one of several reasons: our chromosomes dictate it; our hormones trigger it; our position in the Oedipal triangle of our birth family produces it; or the greater sexed division of human society as a whole (brought on by reproductive differences) leads our psyches down certain predictable pathways that cause us to become women and men.

That these processes don't work in each case to produce an individual with a strong gender identity, a person whose attributes line up neatly with the male or female ideal type, can be attributed to all sorts of bugs in the system without turning to a theory of radical social constructionism. We know that chromosomes and hormones can come in idiosyncratic packets. Maybe something environmental, like an overgrowth of a specific set of brain cells owing to something like the depletion of the ozone layer could produce a whole lot of not-all-there women and men without in any way detracting from the firm and definite nature of the sexes we are supposed to be. Things can go wrong in our family triangle: for example, psychoanalysts have often blamed gender "misfits" on a mother who is too absent or too controlling. Or, as Freud told us, women sometimes get rebellious, running after foolish things like clitoral orgasms that will never truly fulfill them, and they must be reined back in and turned to their proper role in life (which is the only way they can thrive, owing to their basic psychosexual constitution). Or we could all, as a society, lose our way, perhaps by engaging in some foolish social experiment like enjoining androgyny on our children. Think of the potential for not-all-thereness in that! Don't take it from me; read the fevered prose of the far antifeminist right wing, where women are women and men are men, until feminists come along to mess with their heads ... and not incidentally, the ironclad dictates of nature.

This is a discussion in which feminists enthusiastically participate. Many feminists are not social constructionists, and they too seek alternative ways of explaining regularities among people of a single gender as well as those exceptional cases where these regularities fail to hold. For example, the classic liberal feminist explanation for the fact that gender exists but that not everyone fulfills their gender roles perfectly is that we have become collectively confused over what is "sex"—the unchanging biological basis of physiological, psychological, and behavioral dimorphism between men and women—and what is "gender": a particular society's ideas of who men and women should be, what sort of lives they should live, and how they should comport themselves. The first, sex, is relatively permanent. It's physical, with clear psychological correlates. But this only forms the substrate for the second, gender, which can be very silly and arbitrary, not to mention discriminatory and harmful. Fortunately, gender—as opposed to sex—is malleable. Via such means as legislation and consciousness-raising we can scrape off the superfluity of gendered expectations in our culture and leave behind only the "obvious physical differences" and whatever psychological variations arise naturally from them. Once we've reduced femininity and masculinity to their true foundations, then no one, it is thought, will be left fidgeting in a suit of gendered clothes that doesn't fit with their appearance, talents, weaknesses, or sense of themselves.

This has been the most popular feminist rallying cry of the twentieth century, but it has hardly been the only one. Some feminists have disliked liberal feminism because it rests on a very Enlightenment vision of humanity in which all people are atomistic rational agents pursuing their best interests, deserving equal liberty to become who they uniquely are as individuals, irrespective of their sex. Some feminist thinkers question whether "individuals" truly exist as freestanding, liberty-seeking entities. We human beings exist only in the context of our communities, they say, where we are merely a locus for our multiple, shifting identities and relationships. Indeed, some feminists suggest that if we conceive of ourselves as freestanding, liberty-seeking entities, we're simply repeating the mistakes of men, buying into a patriarchal system that has been demonstrably bad for women (and lots of other people too, female and otherwise, like racial and ethnic minorities and lower classes). The last thing we should want to do is be like men, because men have wreaked a lot of havoc in the world.

This is a very impassioned set of debates. Some feminists insist that we shouldn't be stupid and blind: women exist, men exist, they say, and anyone who isn't into playing semantic games can tell the difference between them. We have to work with these differences in any society we want to create. Others are sure that once we can make everyone see that the whole sex/gender categorization is a fantasy, it will cease to have power over us. Better still, we will never get confused again about what is "really real" about sex and what is culturally variable if we see clearly that there's no "really real" to be had.

I think it would be nice to have a notion of gender that encompasses both of these concerns, that has the taste of hard-headed realism and also the savor of a great freedom to innovate. That's not easy; they're sort of contradictory positions. But the good news is that you can choose whatever flavor you prefer and still work together with feminists who believe the opposite. Why? Because the whole exhausting process of arguing over whether sexual difference is biologically based or culturally created, how much and in what proportions, is kind of a red herring. It hardly matters whether there is a biological basis for sex differences, a law of essential maleness and femaleness that's the same in Japan as in Brazil, in Britain as in Gambia, nor does it particularly matter if there are clear regularities of feelings or behavior that occur along gendered lines. It's finally beside the point. Let me try to explain why.

To begin with, at the risk of declaring that the earth is flat, we already know that biological sex differences exist. Human beings, like many other animals, are sexually dimorphic: we come in (at least) two types, and one of each is necessary for reproduction. There are exceptions among us, people who are not clearly one or the other of these two biological types, but they're in the minority. Since these biological differences between women and men extend to some pretty basic things like brain structure, we should not be surprised to learn of psychological and behavioral differences between the sexes that hold cross-culturally.

But the existence of universal, biologically determined sex differences between women and men, even if you imagine that there are a lot of them, don't mean all that much when it comes to deciding what you want to do about them, how relevant they're going to be for your life or my life or our collective social life. This is so for two basic reasons: that we can't know as much about biological sex differences as we might wish, and that what we do know doesn't stack up to an overwhelming obstacle for most of the gender agendas we could imagine pursuing. That is, whatever naturally sexed differences exist, there are also a lot of options for negotiating them.

First, the issue of what we don't know about sex differences: The reason we endlessly climb on the hamster wheel of the nature/nurture debate is because we can argue about it forever without getting anywhere. Scientifically valid answers are not forthcoming. We can't observe people who haven't been influenced by an environment. My friend Pam has identical twin daughters, two girls with the same DNA. You've heard of twin studies, no doubt. Identical twins are a sociobiologist's wet dream. By definition, it would seem, any differences between them must be environmental, not genetic. The kicker, though, is that the environment is complex and present from the moment of conception. You can't effectively control it, subjecting one twin to one environment and the other to another while holding all other variables steady. In the case of Pam's daughters, it's very easy to tell them apart. I've seen fraternal twins that look more similar than they do. In utero, one of them had a big healthy placenta and a sturdy umbilical cord. The other was barely hanging on, with what the doctors called "an umbilical cord no bigger than a scrap of yarn." When the twins were born, prematurely, one weighed less than half as much as the other. Same DNA, different fetal environments, different babies, and today, distinctly different children. Can we really say what differences between them are due to their experiences in utero or their experiences afterward? And what of their similarities? Possibly they're genetic, but maybe they're not; maybe they've had similar environments in certain ways, or different environments that elicited similar reactions in them.

This inability to separate nature and nurture is an in-principle problem. It doesn't mean that there aren't clever ways to work around it, but pulling apart the nature/nurture skein is a great deal more delicate a task than the sound bites on the eleven o'clock news would have you think. Almost anything you want to ask along nature/nurture lines will suffer from this difficulty. Are women more passive than men? Find me a sizable group of precultural females and males, and I'll let you know. Are men physically stronger than women? They appear to be so, but do we know how much of this is due to sex-differentiated diets, exercise, and work patterns, and how much to biological destiny? That's hard to say.

One method of getting at which sex differences are biologically determined is to do cross-cultural research. For example, if men are stronger than women everywhere, that would suggest a biological difference (suggest, but not prove—knowing that a sex difference is universal doesn't tell us that it's biological). Unfortunately, the practice of verifying cross-cultural sex differences in any but the most obvious ways is a tricky business. Trying to describe what women are like in another culture is as tall an order as describing what they're like here at home, where, as we've seen, generalizations about women tend to generate controversy. What people see when they look at a group of women is incredibly biased by what they expect to see, what they hope to see, and what they are afraid of seeing: it goes back to the ratchet in our brains. This is true for trained observers, like anthropologists, and for everyone else as well. For example, I have a friend who does research on evangelical Christian women. These women say that they are not feminists. The message they preach is submission to their husbands, submission even to husbands that are stupid or vile. My friend thinks that a lot of other things take place among these women that contradict their official rhetoric and that evangelical women-only organizations are a place where women get some leverage for themselves over against the men in their lives in what could be interpreted to be a feminist way. Other scholars think she's been taken in, that these evangelical Christian women are the most pathetic sort of dupes of patriarchal society that you could ask for.

Now this is an argument that's going on between a group of highly educated scholars who have all been trained in the same discipline. Imagine if we asked some other observers to take a look at these evangelical Christian women: observers from other countries, of other sexes, other educational backgrounds or social classes. Would they suddenly come to a startling consensus about what's going on with these women? Would they sit down around a table and speak in one voice, saying, "Yes, see how these evangelical women are lending their support to a formal ideology of male dominance, in defiance of their own best interests"? If that's what they all already believed, what they were there to prove to one another, maybe that's what they'd conclude. But that's the only scenario I can imagine that would yield any significant agreement.

This gives some indication about what we don't know about sexual difference, what we're unlikely to be able to pin down definitively. Then there's what we *do* know about sex differences: that when we test for them, even in cultures that have arguably done a lot to magnify their "natural" distribution, we find enormous areas of overlap between women and men. To take a very obvious example, if we plot a chart of men's and women's heights, we will get two bell curves illustrating that men are, on average, taller (see figure 5.1). But the bell curves will overlap. Some women will be taller than most men. Some men will be shorter than most women. Draw a line on the wall representing an individual's height and ask me to guess whether the individual is a woman or a man. Sometimes I'll be right; sometimes I'll be wrong. I'll be right more often when you show me very high or very low marks, but even then there's no guarantee of accuracy. In the much more populous territory in the middle, I'm bound to make a lot of mistakes.

Or take another example: I have read about studies (ones conducted on children, who, it is important to note, have already had several years of socialization as males and females) showing that boys are, on average, 15 percent more aggressive than girls. For the sake of argument, let's say that the researchers know what aggression is and that they know how to measure it accurately. (These are really big assumptions. In actuality, nearly

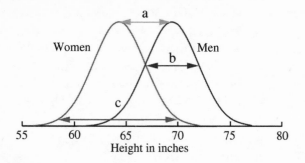

a=difference in height between average woman and average man
b=difference in height among the majority of men
c=difference in height across the spectrum of women

FIGURE 5.1. Differences between average stature of women and men compared with differences in stature across the full population of women. (Statistics from the 2000 Centers for Disease Control report).

half of the studies reported in the classic work in the field, *The Psychology of Sex Differences,* found that aggression did not vary substantially by sex; 5 to 10 percent of the studies found that girls were more aggressive than boys. Many of the studies, including those that found boys to be more aggressive than girls, often had egregious errors in scientific method.) Let's go further to say that this number holds cross-culturally, for both children and adults, that wherever you find human beings of two sexes, you find males being 15 percent more aggressive than females. Call it a verified sex difference if you must. But bear in mind that you still can't decide whether a person is male or female based on how aggressive that person is. There are very aggressive girls and very passive boys hanging out in that overlap between the bell curves.

So far as I am aware, the only sex differences that don't overlap substantially (to the point that differences among members of one sex are much greater than the difference between the averages of each sex) are whether one has XX or XY chromosome configurations, vulvas or penises. Plot these out, and I'm sure you will get a beautiful dumbbell distribution, with a big cluster of females at one end, a big cluster of males at the other end, and a scattering of a few anomalous cases in between.

But then that's what sex *is,* right? We created the categories of sex to account for this precise difference in chromosomal configuration, genitalia, and reproductive role. Of course the categories of sex are going to reflect that difference. What we didn't do was to create categories of sex to account for a differential in people's aggression, or their height, or their mathematical skills, or their nurturing behaviors. These human traits —unlike the distribution of sex chromosomes or the type of external and internal genitalia—have not been shown to be dramatically sex-specific.

This is especially striking when you consider that the people who are trying to measure or discover these comparatively minor sex differences in height or aggression are not people who are trying to prove that men and women are a great deal alike. It's sex *difference* research, not sex *similarity* research. If a similarity emerges in the data, it hardly counts as a finding. It certainly doesn't get reported in the media as a significant new piece of information about the sexes, that we are more alike than we might have thought.

Which brings us to yet another obstacle to discovering which sex differences are universal and/or biologically based and how far they extend. And that is that there is no politically neutral research on sex differences. Every speck of data on sex difference comes trailing misbegotten assumptions and conclusions in its wake. Take the example of aggression in boys once more. We already believe this to be true, that boys are more aggressive than girls, and we even have explanations for why it is true (such as the Darwinian notion that males try to maximize their reproductive success by competing with other males for mates). And we also think we know what this means for society: that boys will be boys, that you can only get so far by telling little Johnny to stop kicking the dog and taking his sister's toys.

Now I was raised by a scientist who cultivated in me deep

sympathies for the way researchers try to work out a puzzle in the pursuit of pure knowledge, only to have the plebeians get hold of their data and make a hash of the whole thing, drawing all sorts of irresponsible conclusions. We're talking about two separate problems here, right? The conclusions of sex difference research—which might be wholly accurate—and the way those conclusions are interpreted and used.

To some extent, yes. But the ideal of a coterie of high-minded scientists abjuring all bias, all social or ethical value, as they quest after pure knowledge is an ideal that is rarely attained. The very fact that researchers (and the people who fund them) are trying to isolate legitimate sex differences indicates a belief that these differences, if discovered, are more socially important than differences between other categories of people that never get this kind of research attention. No one is queuing up to examine differences in mathematical skill between fat people and thin people. Do we think that such a difference exists? I've never heard anyone say so. Would we think it highly important to get this research finding established if such a difference did exist, and if this difference were statistically no more dramatic than that between boys and girls? Probably not. There's not as much at stake there.

There's a lot at stake when it comes to sex differences. We don't just want to find out, in an abstract way, whether boys or girls are on average more likely to be excellent mathematicians, all other things being equal. We want to know what to expect of our children. If girls aren't very good at spatial skills, we want to know that so we can give Jenny a break over how badly she's doing in geometry. We want to know whom to invest in educationally. Why put girls through grueling math courses if they're never going to be very good at math anyway, if their brains aren't optimized to acquire and process this sort of information? We want to know whom to hire for jobs that require mathematical skill. Why look at a dozen applicants if you can be pretty sure that the three female ones aren't up to the task?

No, we don't *have* to use sex difference research this way. Say we get this mythical finding that boys are better than girls at mathematics, that it has always been so and will ever be so. Say that boys are on average 30 percent better at mathematics than girls are (a comparatively large sex difference). Or go all the way with this: say we know what biochemical mechanism is behind this phenomenon of male superiority in mathematics. Say mathematical skill sits on a gene that gets triggered by androgens. Well, we could know all this, draw our overlapping bell curves for mathematical skill in boys and girls, and then conclude that we need to test all our children for mathematical skill so that the odd girl who is a brilliant mathematician doesn't get overlooked, or the odd boy who is as dumb as a fence post when it comes to matters mathematical doesn't get pushed beyond his abilities. Perhaps we could know all this and decide that we need remedial mathematical education for girls, that we should fund a whole new initiative to find out how better to compensate for girls' inborn weakness in this area. Androgen injections for all school-age females! Let no one be left behind because of a treatable biological infirmity!

Knowledge that sex differences exist or do not, and to what degree (recall that in almost all cases, this is knowledge we don't have and are not likely to get in any definitive manner), simply doesn't carry with it a prescription for how these differences should be accommodated socially. Nevertheless, most often the immediate conclusion from sex difference research is that once we have established the existence of certain differences between the sexes, we can henceforth use sex as a shorthand for deciding in advance what an individual is capable of and how they are likely to behave.

What's the problem with this? If it's not obvious, take another example, even more hypothetical. Say that a researcher discovers, as Internet jokes suggest, that women have higher IQs than men do (using, of course, a perfectly accurate measure of something that really exists, that we call "intelligence"). Does this mean that we should decide admittance to Ivy League universities on the basis of sex, with women getting preference? It would sure save time if we could toss out half the applications, wouldn't it?

If one of the boys denied admission because of his sex was my exceptionally bright son, this might really tick me off. It's positively un-American. This isn't how we're supposed to do things. (By the way, in the first version of the classic Stanford-Binet IQ test, girls *did* score significantly higher than boys did. Know what happened? The test designers took this as a sign that there was something wrong with their test, and they went back and tinkered with it until boys reliably scored as well as girls.)

If the results of sex difference research don't provide us with a lot of guidance as to what we should do differently for women and men, girls and boys, then why do we crave the information so badly?

There's an answer that comes to my mind for this: We already prejudge people on the basis of their sex. It's called sexism. Sex difference research just gives us a better warrant for doing it. It makes us feel more righteous in our prejudging, less sexist, and more ... well, more scientific. Like we're talking about facts here, not values. Who can fault us for making generalizations that might lead to unjustified and unethical differential treatment of women and men? We're not setting the agenda here; nature is. Hey, you pissy, nasty feminists—quit your bitching: It's just the *way things are.* Do you get upset when rain falls down instead of up? Do you think you can do something about it by tacking another amendment onto the Bill of Rights? Well, you can't; so live with it. Nature intends certain things for women and men respectively. Better to find out what these intentions are and go with the flow than to keep trying to run up the down escalator.

Of course, we run up the down escalator all the time when it comes to things other than gender. Nature clearly intends for us to live in the dark whenever the sun is not up. Does that stop us from exploiting whatever form of energy we can so that we can be able to see whenever we want to, night or day? Not at all. But heaven forbid that we should apply the same logic to the "natural" roles of women and men.

Oh, it makes me tired. It also reminds me powerfully of another kind of social identity, and the way it used to be, and sometimes still is, "scientifically" justified as the value-neutral judgment of "nature": that is, race. It was not so many years ago that scientists were weighing "Caucasoid" and "Negroid" brains to prove that black folks weren't as smart as white folks (and, guess what, to justify continuing practices of white-superior racism). How foolish to integrate schools, when white people and black people so clearly needed different types of training in order to thrive! We were only being humanitarian when we segregated the races.

Race difference research is very déclassé these days. Try getting a grant from the National Science Foundation to study it. Try reporting its results, ever so neutrally, in the *Washington Post*. Then bury your head, because a huge shitstorm is brewing, and it's headed right at you.

Is the current dearth of race difference research due to an adequate scientific demonstration that there are no significant differences between black and white people to be found, and the subsequent determination that we shouldn't keep wasting our money trying to find them? No. It wasn't like race difference research, when it was done with enthusiasm, kept turning up similarities between black folks and white folks. Oh, they found differences all right. Big ones. Important ones. Ones that justified—or seemed to justify—racist policies.

Was the research done badly? Probably. Were the results accurate? Probably not. But none of this is particularly relevant to why the research stopped. It stopped because we decided that racism was bad. There was a public outcry over it. Racism is not gone, nor are pseudoscientific justifications for it. But the political landscape has changed dramatically where racism is con-

cerned, making it very difficult for people to go around saying
that there are biologically based racial differences (at least when
the putative differences are any more socially combustible than,
say, the finding that African Americans are more prone to sickle-
cell anemia or high blood pressure).

When I was a teenager, a Nobel Prize–winning physics pro-
fessor from Stanford University, William Shockley, analyzed IQ
test results as they differed by race. According to Shockley's survey, Asian Americans were the smartest, followed by European
Americans. African Americans lagged behind. Shockley's research yielded a tsunami of public and scientific reaction. Shockley defended his results tenaciously, primarily by attempting
to prove that the IQ test was a good research tool, that it did
not reflect differences in schooling (i.e., "nurture"), but in some
deeper sort of biologically determined mental ability.

Shockley did not shy away from drawing policy directives
from his research. He did not profess the sort of moral neu-
trality that I have here applied to sex difference researchers in
a benefit-of-the-doubt manner. Shockley advocated voluntary
sterilization for anyone with an IQ under one hundred (which
at that time included the majority of African Americans who
had been tested). On the other end of the IQ spectrum, Shockley offered himself up as a regular donor to the Nobel laureate
sperm bank for the humanitarian cause of helping qualified
women to bear brilliant children like himself.

Predictably, people reacted to Shockley's eugenics proposals
by likening him to Nazi scientists (a libel that Shockley fought
in court, and won, with a cash settlement of exactly one dollar).
But significantly, they reacted every bit as strongly to Shockley's
purported "finding" that there were racial differences in intelligence. What people said to Shockley, over and over again, in one
way or another, was that his results couldn't be true because we
didn't want them to be true. Here we were, trying to move past
our racist heritage and give everyone an equal chance, trying
to go on the assumption that we had been recently taught, that
skin color was only skin deep. Racially based differences in in-

telligence were the last thing we needed to hear about. And so Shockley was shouted down. (This is what happened in public. I'm sure there were millions of racists sitting in their living rooms nodding their heads in agreement with Shockley, thinking he was a brave martyr to a bunch of bleeding-heart liberals that had seized control of the government and media. These racists exist yet today, erecting html monuments to Shockley on the Internet.)

Was Shockley's research flawed? Were his conclusions invalid?

Does it matter? The point is that it was pernicious to be doing that sort of research. However much Shockley may have wished it—and significantly, he didn't—however vehemently he may have argued the point, that research, at that time, could not be politically neutral. It could not be nonracist. The question it asked was a racist one. It rested on the assumption that race might be a significant determining factor of intelligence —something we continue to think relevant to a person's social value. Interestingly, no one became enflamed over Shockley's finding that Asian Americans were smarter than European Americans. It was all about the black/white divide, and why wouldn't it be? That was the most prominent racial divide among Americans. It still is. And Shockley's research threatened to widen it.

Now theoretically, findings like Shockley's could be true, and it wouldn't make a drop of difference. If we weren't busy looking to skin color to reveal something important about people, we would never notice a difference like that in the first place. IQ and race would not be data that were reported on the same form, and the correlations between the two would never be identified. Even if in the course of generalized research on intelligence some computer somewhere popped out the finding that the distribution of intelligence varied by race, that finding wouldn't merit much more than a footnote in a nonracist society.

We don't live in a nonracist society. And we've come to

understand that "data" on racial differences in mental ability or anything else we think valuable are extremely likely to be misused. We doubt our ability to achieve value-neutral findings on race difference. So we leave it alone. I think that's a very smart decision. It doesn't mean that we could never do research on racial differences responsibly. But then, why would we want to?

In the same way, exploring sex differences through ethnography, sociology, psychology, neurology, or any other branch of science is not misguided in principle, and it might yield interesting results. But we have no reason to trust ourselves to do it responsibly right now. On the contrary, we have ample reason to suspect that even when we believe we are inquiring into potential sex differences in a responsible, scientific, open-ended way, we are really just nailing more planks onto a sexist structure.

Maybe one day we will be able to conduct research that demonstrates that women are more nurturing than men without immediately construing this as a justification for leaving women overwhelmingly responsible for child care. Maybe one day we will be able to conduct research that demonstrates that persons with African ethnic roots are more likely to have good rhythm than are persons with European ethnic roots without concluding that blacks belong in vaudeville shows and whites in corporate boardrooms. Of course, if and when that day arrives, we will probably find the idea of isolating these sex or race differences boring and pointless, and we won't bother. In any case, we're not at that point now. We don't lose much—and we stand to gain a lot—by throwing out the baby of sex difference with the bathwater of sexism for the time being: at least until we can trust ourselves to discriminate between the two.

At the outset of this book, I asked for a definition of femaleness that doesn't make women feel inadequate about their femininity, that helps build bridges between feminism and other liberation movements, that is easy to understand, and that accords with our commonsense notions of which people are women and which men. For me, identifying femaleness with the judgment of others—you're a woman if others say you are—meets all these criteria.

Saying that femaleness is in the eye of the beholder (in this case the collective beholder, society) is on the one hand an empirical statement. It's how the world is, it's how a gender determination is actually made, it's the process through which you're handed your female identification card regardless of how "feminine" your feelings, behavior, or even, to some extent, your physiology is. But far more important, drawing an equation between femaleness and the judgment of others is a political statement. It acknowledges that sex as we experience and understand it is inextricably mixed up—at least for now—with sexism. Attributions of sex are about what people can legitimately expect of you and how they can treat you. In the face of this, our first political focus has to be on sex*ism,* not on sex. We can—and I predict with great certainty that we will—continue to talk about sex differences. But as feminists, if we've somehow lost sight of sexism while we've been out exploring the ever-fascinating topic of sex differences, then we need to drag our attention back to what makes the whole issue of sex crucial to feminists: social inequality, its attendant abuses of power, and the harm done to women.

The other helpful thing about locating femaleness in the judgment of others is that people can accept this as a foundation, as the ultimate resting place of gender, while still continuing to believe many more elaborate, complex, and controversial things about gender (such as that femaleness is biologically hardwired, or that it originates in women's relationships with their mothers or the machinations of a capitalist economy or women's roles in reproduction). I'd like to think that no one has to give up their favored notions of gender entirely to adopt the rather radical understanding of gender that I'm presenting here.

I personally gravitate toward the idea that gender and sex are thoroughly socially constructed. But I would never go so far as to say that this is something we *know* about gender. I could be entirely wrong about that. Actually, it wouldn't surprise me to find out that I've erred on the side of attributing almost everything to one end of the pole—social construction—while neglecting the other. But fundamentally, it doesn't matter. Let me say that again: *it doesn't matter.* Because whether gender is biological or socially constructed, absolutely determinative or a barely self-consistent fiction, it's reasonable to both want and expect social change where sex inequality is concerned. If we were to truly learn something verifiable about significant differences between women and men, we need only adjust our theories accordingly and wade back out into the fray.

The truth is, we've never agreed with one another about what constitutes femaleness, but in spite of this, feminists have been capable of a greater public voice and more concerted political action in times past. Perhaps if we can agree that whatever else femaleness is, it is an ascribed identity that is used to discriminate against persons so identified, this will give us the unity necessary to move forward as feminists again.

Biological, cultural, or performed, gender is very, very real. It's about expectations: who will clean the cat box, who will cook dinner, who will drive the children to school? It's about personal safety: who can travel alone, who can live alone, who can walk alone on the streets at night without "courting" violence? It's about paid work: who earns more money, who requires more job flexibility, who will be taken seriously in which professions? So long as we cave into the belief that pay inequity and sexual violence and the whole panoply of instances of gender inequality have something to do with who women and men naturally are (ideas that we persist in holding against the bulk of the evidence), to that extent we will continue to give sexism a free ride.

Am I a woman? Undoubtedly. Am I happy about it? Well, at my age I've come to be more or less happy with who I am, and I am a woman. Does that mean yes? Am I happy to be a member of the sex that bears the next generation? I guess so. It's the reality I've known, and it's been interesting. Am I happy to have the world deciding who I can be and who I ought to be because when they see me coming on the street they can identify me as "a woman"? Not at all. And I like to think that advancing age will never resign me to this.

CHAPTER 6

Why This Matters

Sometimes it's easy to feel that things aren't so bad for women here among white people of a professional class, that we have a lot of power and freedom and don't need to complain so loudly anymore. I've confronted this most with my daughter Sophia, as I've tried to explain to her why I'm a feminist, what feminism is, and why I devote my working life to writing books about it. We've talked about it a lot, yet Sophie still has a hard time grasping the fact that women are systematically oppressed. (I've never tried to put it to her in those exact terms, of course, but that's pretty much the concept I've wanted to get across.) When you look at her world, you can see why it might be a difficult interpretation for her to accept. She sees both her parents working, keeping house, and negotiating to make family decisions; at school, virtually all the authority figures she's in contact with, from teachers to administrators, are women; when something more needs to happen around school, mommies appear on the scene to do it. Women seem very competent, very present in her world. In contrast, the men she knows are mostly boys.

In explaining the need for feminism to Sophie, I've found myself falling back on historical material, stressing how recently it was that women got the right to vote or hold political office or any decent sort of job at all; how not so long ago women were considered property; how there were no team sports for girls when I was in elementary school; how her aunts didn't have bat mitzvahs and her grandmother wasn't even counted as a Jew when it came time to pray.

It's been fairly disturbing to me not to be better able to show

Sophie where, in her world, right now, sexism is located. When Sophie parrots back my words about the history of the oppression of women, they sound thin and unconvincing even to me. It sounds like we're talking about a problem that's in the past.

I was recently at a baby shower where the conversation turned to the question of teaching your children about racism. I brought it up because I've been torn between wanting to tell Sophie just how racist the world is and wanting to let her live just a little longer in the illusion that the color of her friends' skin is no more important than the color of their hair so far as the rest of the world is concerned. ("You know what I've noticed, Mommy?" she asks. "No one in my family has brown skin. Not even my cousins.") On the one hand, it seems somehow racist to let Sophie labor on under the misconception that skin color doesn't count, that it doesn't affect how people are treated. This is something she ought to be learning about, that she ought to be taking into account as she deals with people of different races so that she can better choose the right and sensitive thing to say and do in various situations. But on the other hand, aren't we antiracists trying to achieve a world where skin color *doesn't* count? Right now, Sophie is living there. Why would I dream of purposely moving her to another, not nearly so nice place?

My answer for that, such as it is, has been that African-American children don't have the luxury of not knowing about racism, of bathing in innocent bliss regarding the significance of skin color throughout their long happy childhood years. And if they can't ignore it, why should Sophie? It smells like white privilege to me. So when I was at this baby shower, I started talking with several African-American mothers about what they've taught their children about racism, when, and under what circumstances. These mothers and their children, it is important to note, are living in the same sort of neighborhoods as we do, attending the same schools, working the same sort of jobs—in short, occupying the same social strata. But what they said shocked me. For the most part, they haven't told their chil-

dren about racism. They don't want to have to talk about it until it comes up, and so far it hasn't come up in any way that they
haven't been able to paper over. To the extent that they have
talked about it, it's been in a historical way: they've read their
children upbeat books about the history of the slave trade and
how it ended and how the civil rights movement fixed all the
problems (like segregation) that lingered on. These mothers said
that they've even surprised themselves as they've told their children that it's all different now, that things are much better now.
Because these women suffer no illusions about the very real
presence of racism in American society today. How could they?

I was surprised, but I guess I shouldn't have been. Have I ever
sat Sophie down and told her about the Holocaust, in which
scores of members of her extended family were systematically
murdered? Absolutely not. I live in fear of the day that it comes
up. In fact, I wouldn't let her watch *The Sound of Music* until I
remembered that during the course of the movie the evil Nazis
from whom the von Trapp family escaped were only invading
Austria, not gassing Jews.

Why don't I want to get into this with Sophie? Because I
don't want her thinking that people could want to kill her just
because she's Jewish, and furthermore, that this precise thing
happened to a lot of Jews in an extremely gruesome way very recently. In other words, my instinct to rear Sophie as a sensitive,
politically aware person has warred with my desire to make her
feel safe and protected, and there's no question which has won
so far. Of course, she's only six years old. I imagine things will
change.

I guess what's more surprising to me about all this isn't that
we've wanted to protect our children from harsh realities regarding racism, anti-Semitism, and sexism, but that we've been
able to. Does this mean that these realities don't exist in our en-
lightened little subculture? That we are so free from these dread-
ful "isms" that we can only explain them to our children by
saying they're over and done with? In the Jim Crow South, neither black nor white children could altogether miss that there

was some serious racial stuff going on, not for the first six years of their lives. Are things so drastically improved now that we can afford to behave as though these isms don't affect our lives? Is racism confined to the inner city, sexism to Afghanistan? Is it time to proclaim that sexism is mainly a thing of the past in America and that our primary task now is simply continued vigilance against its return? I can't tell you how wrong this sounds to me.

Yesterday as I was enjoying my breakfast, a man came over to my table and started hitting on me. He was leaning in, looking at my breasts, slowing his voice into an insinuating drawl, saying silly things like "I bet you like to be comfortable ... *real* comfortable." This happens so extremely rarely these days that quite honestly it took me a long time to figure out that he was coming on to me. It didn't occur to me that he actually meant it until he said, "Okay, you, me, up to your office right now. I won't tell my wife and you won't tell your husband."

Then and there, without the slightest effort, I found myself back in a set of behaviors that I haven't used in years. It was like riding a bicycle. You act nice. Because you don't want to hurt his feelings. You indicate that this isn't something you're interested in, no offense intended.

Now why did I have to act nice? Why did I have to spare his feelings? Was I just being kind to a fellow human being? No harm in that, certainly. And maybe that's all it was. But it did cross my mind, in an instant of reflex, that maybe he would start following me around saying nasty things to me if I wasn't careful not to offend him; maybe he would rape me. Which, just like in the bad old days when this kind of encounter happened much more frequently, makes for a nervous little dance. You have to be nice, so as not to anger them. But if you're too nice, they think you're encouraging them, and then you have to say no in a more obvious way. Then they're *really* mad, because now you've "led them on." At what point do they decide that you're playing games with them and that they should just take what you are so clearly (to them) offering?

For all its novelty in my life now as an over-forty matron, the attention from this man wasn't flattering, let me assure you. All I could think of was how awful it would be if I couldn't go back to my favorite breakfast place. Now if this is how beleaguered and intimidated a middle-aged bad-tempered feminist can feel over an inept sexual proposition by a guy who seems comparatively harmless, then I don't think we've attained gender utopia. Nor do I think that all is right in River City when my three-year-old daughter comes home from day care and says, "Mom, I think my thighs are too fat, right here," as she pinches her slim, sturdy leg.

I could go on and on about life on the home front, but I'd rather widen the lens a bit. We are not living in a place where gender is insignificant when only 14 percent of the United States Congress is female. This is not, you can be sure, the result of some statistical fluke associated with electing only the best-qualified individuals to public office. We rank well behind Sweden in female political representation (at 45 percent) and Denmark (at 38 percent). Of course, we've all heard the rumors that the Nordic states are some sort of rare and wonderful gender paradise. However, we're also well behind Costa Rica, Mozambique, Vietnam, Bulgaria, Rwanda, Tanzania, and Mexico when it comes to having women as elected representatives. In fact, we rank fifty-ninth out of roughly 161 countries for whom statistics are reported.

Things are not better in the corporate world. Women compose 46.5 percent of the United States labor force and represent 49.5 percent of those in managerial or professional specialty positions: that is, in positions linked to the direct exercise of corporate power. But at the higher levels of corporate America, up at the top of the Fortune 500 companies, there's only one woman for every nine men. Corporate officers are 12.5 percent female, but only 6.2 percent have titles like "chairman," "vice-chairman," "president," or "CEO." As of 2000, there are still only two female CEOs among the Fortune 500 companies, while ninety companies out of the five hundred have no female corporate officers at all. In dollars and cents, women's lot is even worse: only 4.1 percent of "top earners" are female, and more than 83 percent of Fortune 500 companies count no females among their five highest-earning officers.

That's how women are fitting in at the most elite levels. They're more populous, but not necessarily better off, at less elite levels. Though the statistic varies a bit from year to year, for some time now women have been earning approximately seventy-five cents to a man's dollar. Women are concentrated in lower-paying professions. (Or maybe these professions are lower-paying because women are concentrated in them.) Within a traditionally prestigious profession, like teaching, for example, there are fewer and fewer women the higher up one goes in the educational system: kindergarten teachers are almost all women while college teachers are more likely to be men; many women are teachers, but comparatively few are principals and presidents. Harder to quantify, but nevertheless important in most women's lives, is the phenomenon known as "the second shift": even in dual-career couples, wives spend proportionately more time—about twice as much—performing housework and child care tasks. If all that tidying becomes too onerous and a woman decides to end her marriage, she will have to bear in mind that when couples divorce, men do better financially than do their former wives, usually by quite a bit, and that fully 46 percent of single mothers live in poverty (as contrasted to 9 percent of two-parent families). Indeed, worldwide, two-thirds of those living in poverty are women.

Meanwhile, a woman's right to choose whether or not to give over nine months of her life to having a baby she doesn't want is under constant attack. Though abortion is still "safe and legal" in the United States, access to it has been limited in a number of ways over the past three decades since abortion first came under the protection of federal law. Chances are your employer's insurance plan doesn't cover the cost of your abortion; Medicare definitely won't, and don't even dream that the United States armed forces will take care of your little problem if you're

in their employ. Mature middle-class women are still able to secure abortions when needed, but then their rate of unplanned
pregnancy is considerably lower than that of younger, poorer
women, who are much more likely to make the decision to raise
another human being to adulthood based on the immediate
availability (or not) of a few hundred dollars. Depending on
what state you live in, you may also be subject to parental con-
sent or notification laws, or requirements for counseling and a
waiting period before receiving your safe and legal abortion.

Then there are the ever-present realities of domestic violence and rape to consider. According to some studies, up to 35
percent of women admitted to hospital emergency rooms are
there as a result of domestic violence. When you consider all the
other things that might bring you to an emergency room—
car accident, asthma attack, severe stomach flu, sprained ankle
from a slip on an icy sidewalk—this is a high number indeed.
The United States Department of Justice reported in 1998 that
women experienced at least nine hundred thousand violent
offenses at the hands of a husband, boyfriend, or ex-boyfriend.
That's roughly 2 percent of the female population in any given
year, or an estimated 25 to 35 percent of adult women who over
the course of their lifetimes experience domestic violence.
(Men are assaulted by intimate partners too, more than you
might suspect, but not as frequently or as lethally. Women are
abused about five times more often than men.) If you're a
woman looking to lower your chances of getting murdered,
you'd be best advised to give up an active sexual and romantic
life: 33 percent of women who are murdered are killed by an intimate partner.

The Centers for Disease Control estimate that 683,000 rapes
occur every year in the United States, though no more than 16
percent of these are reported. Younger women and girls are dis-
proportionately affected: more than half the rapes women suffer
in their lifetimes happen before the age of eighteen, and a third
occur before the age of twelve. Fully 28 percent of college
women have had an experience of rape or attempted rape, and

nearly one in ten college men admit to having engaged in aggressive sexual behavior that met the legal definition of rape.

It's true that in many arenas sexism tends to come in more insidious, less easily denounced packages than it did a couple of generations ago. When I ask my students what sets their feminist ire to burning, obviously they no longer point to an inability for women to vote or own property, or even to a feminine mystique that glorifies housewifely perfection above all else. Usually they want to talk about the media instead: about magazines for teenage girls that concentrate on losing weight, getting boys to notice them, and getting a date to the prom, and women's magazines that concentrate on losing weight, getting men to notice them, and finding a husband. Eating disorders are positively epidemic among young women. If medical studies regard their etiology as multiple and complex, most of the women I hear talking about this think there's only one cause worth mentioning: an absolutely relentless pressure to be thin, spearheaded by the media, and a corresponding pressure to react to any amount of perceived pudge with a punishing course of body disciplines including dieting, exercise, and self-induced vomiting. Indeed, one of my students, Bonnie, tells me that she has a niece who is five feet six inches tall, weighs eighty pounds, and doesn't allow fat to cross her lips. This would probably read as just another sad case of teenage self-starvation, except that her niece is autistic and suffers from motor deficiencies and learning disabilities. As Bonnie remarks, "A lot doesn't get through to her, but *that*"—the pressure to be thin—"got through."

Young women also complain that the sexual double standard lives on: you're a virgin or a slut, and neither of these are good things to be. When Britney Spears was a virgin, she was a joke in many quarters. You know ... former Mouseketeer, prissy little good girl. Now Britney is a slut—at least to judge from her fashion choices—but she's still a joke, just in a different way. Another student, Cindy, remembers being a fan of the singer Shakira when she was recording exclusively for the Spanish-language market. When Shakira crossed over to the mainstream,

Cindy didn't recognize her at first. Somehow in the transition Shakira had become thin and blond and had a perky new set of breasts. Why, one has to wonder, is brazen sexual display of one's slim, toned body (and preferably, one's blond locks) the only way to illustrate to the world that one has "grown up" or "become a woman"? Only sexual availability signals adulthood? Recently the news media reported that for teenagers "safe sex" has been more or less translated into oral sex, which is apparently thought to be a less disease-spreading activity than sexual intercourse. But there's a catch: only boys are on the receiving end. Somehow this doesn't sound like the delectable fruits of the sexual revolution I grew up hearing so much about.

People rarely describe such things in terms of the sexual victimization of girls and women. Why? Well, aren't girls choosing all this? Who is coercing them? What villainous powers are acting to limit their opportunities? If anything, teenage anorexia and bulimia, and even fellatio, are only signs of female stupidity, since presumably all these girls and young women who are starving themselves and giving out hummers with nothing expected in return could instead be making more self-affirming, life-affirming, woman-affirming choices.

Among adult women the issues are somewhat different, but again, they are assumed to be the result of free choice. For example, women in my town often end up in the unpaid labor force, caring for their homes and children, while their husbands, who used to share a similar career status with their wives, go clambering up the ladder of professional and financial success. But women *choose* this, right? To take advantage of the luxury afforded to them by their economic class of being home with their children? Also, like younger women, the women of my acquaintance spend enormous amounts of mental and emotional energy worrying about how obscenely fat they believe themselves to be. But who is "making" women do this? Isn't this our own fault?

If you ask me whether I'd rather live in Saudi Arabia, where I couldn't drive a car, or here, I'll choose here every time, even if it means taking seventy-five cents to a man's dollar and endlessly obsessing over ten "excess" pounds of abdominal fat. It's true that there's a certain amount of choice involved in femaleness here in the United States that we didn't have historically and that is still absent in many parts of the world. Still, I don't think it's an accident or a choice, either one, that women earn less, attain less, worry more about their appearance, and are more often the objects of sexual violence than men. There are a lot of pressures operating here, reasons why women "choose" the arguably less life-enhancing path.

For most of this book, I've been bemoaning the anxiety associated with sensing, in a variety of ways, that I haven't been an adequate woman, that I haven't measured up. I think this is manifestly not the most destructive thing sexism does—that it causes privileged women like me to feel self-loathing in relation to our apparently substandard femaleness—especially when you consider that we enjoy continuing entitlements associated with being white and female (like having the men close to us believe that they should support us financially) at the same time that we reap the benefits of the rather stunning successes of the second wave of the feminist movement that have provided us with unprecedented opportunities for professional success and personal fulfillment.

But just because it's not necessarily the most destructive thing that is done with ideas about femaleness and maleness does not mean that the crushing of spirits isn't a real harm associated with the strongly sex-differentiated environment in which we live. Everyone's pain is real, even if it seems shallow and narcissistic to others, and the pain of feeling that you aren't living up to an identity you can't change is significant. And unlike many forms of gender inequality, this is a cost that is borne by women and men alike.

I recently read an article titled "Like a Virgin," by a man named John Weir. It was about how the author, at age thirty-six, decided that he wanted to have sex with a woman. He had had plenty of sexual experience with men, but nothing with women past a little groping when he was in college. So he set out to find a woman to sleep with, a quest he pursued on both coasts. He flirted at parties and in bars. He was really making time with the ladies; he found it surprisingly easy to engage their interest. But ultimately, he felt he couldn't seduce any of these women. He thought he would be doing so under false pretenses, and that that would be wrong. He finally decided that he'd have to hire a prostitute, and so he and his straight friend Nick went to a Manhattan brothel. There John fulfilled his goal of having sex with a woman. The woman's name was Heather. John thought that Heather was very beautiful with her clothes off. He thought that sex with Heather was all right. Interesting. Different from sex with a man, and yet not so different after all. Afterward, he and Nick went out for cheese fries. Nick heartily congratulated John for performing oral sex on Heather and offered him more fries, apparently as a reward. John concluded his story by saying, "It's not women I want. I don't even really want men. What I want is that unquestioned ease in the world, like Nick flirting with the waitress without caring about his awkwardness or real-izing his grace. I want a woman so I can see myself, even briefly, even just in Nick's eyes, as a man."

This story made me very sad. Mostly because it reminded me strongly of my friend George. George had sex with men and women, though he mostly thought of himself as gay. He died of AIDS when he was thirty-seven years old. George was a closet case, a subject we discussed endlessly. He was dissatisfied with having to choose between two worlds, both of which he found repugnant: that of heterosexuality, where he couldn't have sex with men, not ever, and where he'd be expected to support a wife and children and work at a salaried job his whole life; and that of homosexuality, where everyone would think they knew all about who he was just because he said he was "gay." George didn't want to buy Barbra Streisand records or frame Calvin Klein underwear ads to put on his wall, and he didn't want any-one expecting him to.

George never did solve this conundrum. He tried and tried to figure out why he wanted to have sex with men, since it seemed to him that his life would be so much simpler if he could just be straight. He told me that sex with women felt better, that it provided a more pleasurable set of physical sensations. But he never experienced the same craving to have sex with women that he felt where men were concerned. From the time he was in college, he used to tell me, "I think it's because I never had good male friends when I was in high school. My friends were all girls." George was very popular in high school. He was handsome and smart, he was senior class president, and he went to the prom with a real knockout, the perfect blond-haired, blue-eyed California girl that all the other guys coveted. But he didn't play football, and he didn't drink beer with the other guys, and these felt like terrible lacks to George, sure signs of his inadequacy as a man. He told me again and again that the actual sex he had with men was more or less incidental, that what he wanted was to feel accepted as a man, to be with another guy and feel connected.

The point is not that if only George hadn't had to face down a set of masculine gender stereotypes that ill suited him, then he never would have been driven to having sex with other men. Honestly, whatever he believed about himself, I don't think George was sleeping with men as part of a confused attempt to feel more manly. I think George was gay, period, but so conflicted about it that he felt driven to rationalize it in all sorts of circuitous psychological ways. Nevertheless, I was deeply sympathetic to George's fundamental plight: that when he placed himself alongside an ideal of masculine perfection, he felt that he fell miserably short, and that he desperately wanted to be regarded as a person, not as a sexual orientation.

There's something really pitiful about us all judging ourselves against ideals of femininity and masculinity that, in my opinion, we've mostly invented out of whole cloth (or which, at the least, don't truly come "naturally" to most of us, but have to be trained in). If we really feel compelled to measure ourselves against some standard so we can bemoan how unworthy we are, the least we could do is pick out something less trifling than our percentage of body fat or the width of our shoulders.

Pushing people into gendered categories is a bad business, making for a lot of unhappiness at the same time that it's underwriting a system of deep social (sexed, gendered) inequalities. But can we do without it?

I've drawn a lot of parallels to race, but sex and race are not exactly the same. You could imagine race disappearing at some point in the future. Not only coming to be less significant, or ceasing to be an axis of social inequality, but truly disappearing. Sufficient miscegenation would produce a whole world full of people with that lovely deep dark tan that was considered the height of attractiveness when I was a child (and is now believed to be a prescription for malignant melanoma among white people). It wouldn't just be a handful of folks who could "pass." Everyone would pass for human, and that would be that. This is extremely unlikely to happen with sex. It hasn't happened with any other primates, not even any other mammals. It would take some major genetic engineering or a really bizarre set of mutations to eliminate human sexual dimorphism and replace it with some other means of reproduction.

But could we recognize sex differences to one extent or another and nevertheless decide to live as though people are people, deserving of a certain amount of respect and personal choice regardless of what part they (can or do) play in reproducing the species? I don't know. I feel confident that we can do better than we're doing now. As for the rest, we won't know until we try.

NOTES

1. What Is a Woman?

Page 17: Sojourner Truth's speech was delivered in 1851, before the advent of audio recordings. The version here—the one most commonly quoted— is taken from the memory of Matilda Joslyn Gage. Gage was present at the lecture but apparently did not commit it to writing until 1863. Newspaper accounts from 1851 record a speech with similar content but without the repeated phrase "ain't I a woman?"

3. Feeling for Others: Women and Emotion

Page 62: On the Princeton study of smiling as an indication of sexual interest, see Peggy O'Crowley, "When I See You Smile," *Newark Star-Ledger*, 17 February 2002, section 2, page 2.

Page 63: The magazine article profiling "The World's Sexiest Athletes" was by David A. Keeps and appeared in *Us Magazine*, 28 January 2002, pp. 42–47.

4. Walking the Walk: Acting Like a Woman

Page 91: The quote from Karl Sabbagh can be found in Russell Chandler, *Understanding the New Age* (Dallas: Word Publishing, 1988), 240.

5. Who's Looking? The Judgment of Others

Page 97: On the possible historical recentness of systems of social inequality, see, for example, Andrew Sherratt, "Mobile Resources: Settlement and Exchange in Early Agricultural Europe," in *Ranking, Resource, and Exchange*, C. Renfrew and S. Shennan, eds. (Cambridge: Cambridge University Press, 1982), 13.

Page 98: The quote from W. E. B. Du Bois can be found in Kwame Anthony Appiah, *In My Father's House: Africa in the Philosophy of Culture* (New York: Oxford University Press, 1992), 41.

Page 112: *The Psychology of Sex Differences* is by Eleanor Maccoby and Carol Nagy Jacklin (Stanford, Calif.: Stanford University Press, 1974). A thorough discussion of potential errors in these studies can be found in Anne Fausto-Sterling, *Myths of Gender* (New York: Basic Books, 1992), chap. 5.

Page 116: On the initial sex discrepancy in IQ scores on the Stanford-Binet test, see Georgia Earnest García and P. David Pearson, "Assessment and Diversity," in *Review of Research in Education,* vol. 20, edited by Linda Darling-Hammond (Washington, D.C.: American Educational Research Association, 1994), 340.

6. Why This Matters

Page 128: Statistics on women's representation in national parliaments can be found in Inter-Parliamentary Union, "Women in National Parliaments," 25 October 2002 (http://www.ipu.org/wmn-e/classif.htm).

Pages 128–29: Statistics on women's representation in the leadership of Fortune 500 companies can be found in Catalyst, "200 Catalyst Census of Women Corporate Officers and Top Earners of the Fortune 500" (http://www.catalystwomen.org/press_room/factsheets/factscoteoo.htm). Catalyst is a "nonprofit research and advisory organization working to advance women in business and the professions."

Page 129: Detailed statistics on women's income and employment are available from the U.S. Census Bureau. The statistics on the poverty of single mothers are from 1993; the statistics on world poverty are from the United Nations. The benchmark study of women's disproportionate housework in dual-career families is *The Second Shift* by Arlie Hochshild (New York: Avon Books, 1997).

Page 130: On domestic violence, see J. Massey, "Domestic Violence in Neurologic Practice," *Archives in Neurology* 56 (1999): 659–60; M. Rennison and W. Welchans, *Intimate Partner Violence* (Washington, D.C.: U.S. Department of Justice, Office of Justice Programs, Bureau of Justice Statistics, May 2000).

Pages 130–31: Statistics on rape rates are from the Centers for Disease Control, "Sexual Violence," *Injury Fact Book 2001–2002* (Atlanta, Ga.: Centers for Disease Control, 2002) (http://www.cdc.gov/ncipc/fact_book/ 24_Sexual_Violence.htm).

Pages 133–34: John Weir's article, "Like a Virgin," can be found in *PoMoSexuals,* edited by Carol Queen and Lawrence Schimel (San Francisco: Cleis Press, 1997), 52.

ACKNOWLEDGMENTS

I wrote this entire book, so I will take credit—and blame—as head chef. But there were many, many cooks in the kitchen with me, tasting it chapter by chapter and offering much-needed and much-appreciated criticism and encouragement. Among those who read and commented upon the entire manuscript were Lauren Bryant, Marlin Eller, Grey Gundaker, Reed Malcolm, Susan Greene, Arlene Stein, Bonnie Greenberg, Maya Poran, Susan Lee, Elizabeth Reis, Tom McGee, Kerry Dennehy, Jesse Carliner, Marie Papageorgis, Robert Spero, Faulkner Fox, Teresa Shaw, Sylvia Wolfe, Jon Greene, Jody Shapiro, and Stephen Moore. Additional assistance with individual chapters and the book proposal came from Keyana Rogers, Carla Petievich, Aditya Adarkar, José Cabezón, Kathryn Carliner, Elizabeth Pullen, Carolyn McGee, Jane Hurwitz, Deborah Campbell, David Benfield, Marion Grau, Jeffrey Groves, Beth Say, Elisabeth Mayfield, and Nancy Solomon (who also came up with the subtitle). They didn't all like the book, but they persevered in liking me, and I am especially grateful for that.

My students at Montclair State University were cheerful in the face of my endless attempts to use them for market research. They voted on titles, subtitles, and jacket designs as the project neared completion. Students in my Feminist Theory class read the entire manuscript as well, offering a valued perspective. My colleagues in the Philosophy and Religion Department— Stephen Johnson, Michael Kogan, Lise Vail, David Benfield, Roland Garrett, and Chris Hererra—were also ready to serve as a mini-focus group whenever the occasion merited it, and their comments were pertinent and insightful. Assistance with my questions on genetics came from Gill Diamond, and last-minute research was helped along by Robert and Sylvia Wolfe. Ferdous Gheyas and John Tonry lent their computer graphing skills to the illustrations. I'm grateful indeed to all the folks at Hot Bagels Abroad—Ayman Ahmed, Nasser Ali, Hany Ahmed, Teresa Flores, Maria Quintanilla, Steve Karl, Jen Sery, Amira Hajismaiel, Paulino Bravo, Veronica Colonna, and Kayla King—who fed me every morning and gave me a warm place to work.

Amy Caldwell of Beacon Press continues to be all one could hope for in an editor: sharp, savvy, and enthusiastic and hard-headed in turns as those qualities are required. Martin Rowe helped me to find my agent, Nancy Ellis, who was instantly up to speed as the book was ready to go to press. As copyeditor, Mary Ray Worley combined precision and enthusiasm in equal measure. Thanks to Christina Spatz, Laura Clayton Furst, and Lori Krafte for proofreading, and to Sarah Gillis of Beacon Press for production assistance.

I owe a special debt of gratitude to Susan Lee, who told me that this was the book I needed to write next. I'm quite sure I never would have had the idea without her provocation, and if I had, I certainly wouldn't have acted on it. In the debts overdue column go thanks to my college mentor, John G. Tomlinson, who was the first person to convince me that writing skills are transferable across different genres, and that boldness in one's creative undertakings is absolutely mandatory, since one will be dead a long time and any failure or embarrassment is likely to go with one. This project, like all I've undertaken, has been greatly aided by the friendship of Teresa Shaw, who has been consistently willing to step in and run interference for me, ever since one memorable February evening in 1979 in a hotel room in Cairo.

Jonathan Greene gives me time and space and laughter (and food and lodging), which are all any writer really needs. I am continually awed by my good fortune in successfully engaging him as my partner in life and parenting. My thanks to Delores O'Neil, Leona Palmer, May Butler, Tracy Epps, Maryis Villada,

Ruthy Tannis, Poché Hill, Aalilyah Graham, Surayyah Wolfe, Emah LaBoy, Ruth Banks, Tony Earl, Dandrea Palmer, Carmen Bernal, and Janna Toodle, who brought my daughter Lucy from the nine-to-twelve-month-old who appears in these pages to the two-and-a-half-year-old she is today. Any degree of social acceptability that Lucy has mastered is owing to their kind ministrations.

Lucy herself is both a diversion and an inspiration. Watching her train the laser beam of her attention on life's little mysteries gives everyone around her a new appreciation of them. Sophie has matured from the little girl who sneered at Barbie but would only wear dresses into a true intellectual companion. Her take on everything from fashion to fluid mechanics to theology is always intriguing, and her company is truly a blessing.

I dedicate this book to my daughters, and to everyone's daughters and sons, in the hope that they can create a world where gender matters less and humanity matters more.

INDEX

O circ
11-16-05